The View
from the States

The View
from the States

National Politics in Local
Newspaper Editorials

Jan P. Vermeer

ROWMAN & LITTLEFIELD PUBLISHERS, INC.
Lanham • Boulder • New York • Oxford

ROWMAN & LITTLEFIELD PUBLISHERS, INC.

Published in the United States of America
by Rowman & Littlefield Publishers, Inc.
A Member of the Rowman & Littlefield Publishing Group
4720 Boston Way, Lanham, Maryland 20706
www.rowmanlittlefield.com

12 Hid's Copse Road
Cumnor Hill, Oxford OX2 9JJ, England

British Library Cataloguing in Publication Information Available

Library of Congress Cataloging-in-Publication Data

Vermeer, Jan Pons.
    The view from the states : national politics in local newspaper
editorials / Jan P. Vermeer.
        p. cm.
Includes bibliographical references (p.) and index.
    ISBN 0-8476-8652-3 (alk. paper)—ISBN 0-8476-8653-1 (pbk. : alk.
paper)
    1. Editorials—United States. 2. United States—Politics and
government. I. Title.
    PN4784.E28 V47 2002
    070.4'42—dc21
                                                          2002001791

Printed in the United States of America

♾™ The paper used in this publication meets the minimum requirements of
American National Standard for Information Sciences—Permanence of Paper for
Printed Library Materials, ANSI/NISO Z39.48-1992.

STORY-TELLING, OK, but
what the big picture??

In memory of my parents,
Helena Maria and Cornelis Vermeer,
and with respect for
Robert and Joan Wallick.

1) lot of long + boring info, qualitative,
sort of vague, but upfront about it (pg (5)

2) Some interesting, tble 3.3 unclear
pg 33, ok lot of local variation pg 34) Variation &
that interesting. It's somewhat local but (35) not
exclusively. 36 and its more policy driven
than at. Jas See

3) Congress, editors seem to reflect public - but
CHAIN | what about ideology??
WHERE IT | writtten, like local member. What about ideology??
ONES | Although N'd of Helios?? Why a positive to local
of friends?? 4?) Why so blind about local goal??
In general I felt feeling less optimistic than
conclusion

4) Kind of a long story into a
73) Interesting - suggestion about
a I milleniums 76) But need
to generalize more !!

57 Similar to Cong.

Interesting that, again, that editorial might lead to public bad perception of ~~bureau~~. $371
bureau.

GREATER SPECIFICS !! PG 93

6) SC PART CONFUSING TO
    EDITORS (105) AND
INTERESTING (106)   TABLE 107 !!

MODERATE CT ?? TIME BOUND ??

7)
   PORK & SELF. INTEREST

Contents

Tables

Preface

As inconceivable as the events of September 11, 2001, were before they occurred, it seems just as unimaginable that any element of the American political system would be unchanged afterwards. The differences in the post-attack nation strike most citizens as profound and far-reaching. Patriotism evidenced by flags, ceremonies, and heartfelt singing of the "Star Spangled Banner" at sports events rose to heights not seen for forty years. President George W. Bush's popularity outpaced even his father's high-water mark set during the Gulf War. Increased airport security and special precautions taken during the Super Bowl and the Winter Olympics caused minor but well-tolerated inconveniences for travelers and spectators. The "War on Terrorism" at home and abroad, it would seem, changed the fabric of the nation.

Not everything has changed, however. Exceptional events evoke exceptional responses and cause unexpected departures from normal behavior. Nevertheless, underlying patterns that guide our actions and influence our choices usually persist—or reemerge after a time. In order to understand the disruption caused by the terrorist attack on the United States, we also need to know what normal ways of acting are. Only then can we see what has been altered and what has stayed the same. The clear implication is that we must know what is "usual" before we can identify the "unusual."

The patterns of editorial content described in this book present a case in point. In 1994, editors commented on a wide range of issues in what seems, in comparison, to be calm times. Even then, however, substantial numbers of editorials dealt with national and international issues. Given the increased salience of events around the world and in Washington, D.C., one would expect even greater attention being paid to national political affairs. Editors are in part "news-driven" in their selection of topics for commentary, and the impetus to write about decisions in the nation's capital has to have been greater since September 11 than it was in 1994. It is an expectation readily derived from the research reported in the pages that follow. Although the Haiti situation, for instance, was a great deal less threatening, to put it mildly, than the events of September 2001, nine out of ten editors devoted one or more editorials to it. One would expect even more such choices now. National news has become more salient than ever.

More specifically, the chapter on editorial commentary on Congress suggests that editors want Congress to respond to presidential initiatives rather than to develop policy on their own. That "handmaiden" to the president role we can readily see in the news coverage in the months since September 2001. News focus centered on the White House and Congress serves as a sounding board and a mechanism for correcting any errors that presidential proposals may have included. That pattern is amply documented in chapter 3.

We would further expect current editorial commentary to emphasize local tie-ins and contributions made by local political leaders. It is a basic conclusion of this book that editorial commentary interprets national politics in local terms. That impetus can be expected to be as strong as ever. Editors serve local readers by drawing the connections between their concerns and the world around them.

National political affairs look different from the perspective of the states because local editors frequently interpret national developments in terms of state and local concerns. Whereas the national press find national politics significant enough to devote editorials to for its own sake, local daily newspaper editors frequently justify their attention to national matters by connecting them to subjects of interest at home. As a result, readers of local newspaper editorials see national politics through the prism of state and local issues.

Editors are not objective—by design, they take sides, they criticize and evaluate, and they show favoritism. Nevertheless, they are still journalists, and their choices resemble the choices reporters make in covering the news. What is important, what is of interest, and what affects the readers deserves commentary. September 11, 2001, did not change that. But it did change the importance and relevance of national politics to local editors. Knowing how those editors typically responded to national affairs gives us a baseline for judging what has changed and what has not.

My assumption is that editorials affect local public discourse on matters of concern in the paper's circulation area. The newspapers' editorials on national events and institutions then have the potential of influencing not only how individuals think about the national affairs, but also how significant participants in the local conversations about these issues approach them. If these editorials approach national concerns through connections to local interests, then public discourse on national political affairs may potentially reflect that perspective, including local discourse on the direction the nation should take in the wake of the threats of terrorism.

The book's argument is supported by evidence derived from a reading of every editorial published in 1994 in ten local daily newspapers from across the nation. Each region of the nation is represented in the selection. By design, newspapers with circulation centered around a locality, rather than a region or wider, were selected. Because I examined every editorial in these papers over the course of the year, I was able to discern connections drawn to national politics in editorials that otherwise were devoted to state and local affairs. By contrast, had I restricted myself to editorials addressing national and international affairs only, I would have missed a great deal of the total picture.

Gathering these editorials required the assistance of many people. I am indebted to a number of colleagues who found individuals willing to photocopy the editorials for me, and all did a commendable job. For two newspapers, page numbers for the pages on which the editorials were published were not provided. But since editorials appear on the editorial page in virtually the same location every day, anyone interested in finding an editorial cited from these two papers will have no difficulty locating it, even without the page number. For their assistance I would like to thank Thad Beyle, Brad Canon, Julie Clark, Catherine Davies, Richard Francis, Michelle Garza, Kevin Hanken, Kirk Haverkamp, Jay Houts, Steven Lacy, Justin Orbock, Scott Peters, Joe Stewart, Dennis Wakefield, Diane Wall, Stephen Wasby, Darrell West, and Freeman Wright.

Financial assistance, which I gratefully acknowledge, came from a Goldsmith Research Award from the Joan Shorenstein Barone Center on the Press, Politics and Public Policy at Harvard University. I benefited, too, from spending most of the fall semester of 1997 as a Visiting Scholar at the Ray C. Bliss Institute for Practical Politics at the University of Akron. John C. Green provided the opportunity, Steve Brooks made the visit possible and did everything he could to make the stay enjoyable, Rick Farmer graciously shared his office (and many of his lunch hours) with me, and Bill Lyons opened his home to me for the time I was there. To all I owe many thanks.

Here at Nebraska Wesleyan, the help many student office workers over the years gave me in this project, including Amy Duval, Amy Berg, Meg Allen, and Amanda Schneider, among others, proved indispensable. Secretarial assistance from Rhonda Lakey was worth more than she knows, and Pat Ullrich was also helpful at the very last stages. Of course, my colleagues, Kelly Eaton and Bob Oberst, who both know what it takes to publish at a teaching institution, recognized my preoccupation with this project over the years and made due allowances. Thanks to all.

My sister, Trudy V. Selleck, has been a long-distance source of strength and support. She will see her own professional work come to fruition, also, I am sure.

Some people, including myself at times, thought this book would never be finished: the skeptics were wrong, the optimists were right. I thank Mary Carpenter at Rowman & Littlefield for sticking with me through the project, and Jason Proetorius for coordinating production. I am also grateful for the copyediting and proofreading work that Brigitte Scott and Judy Fernow performed on the manuscript as it moved from my computer to the final product.

To all who have helped along the way, I extend my gratitude. While I wish there were no errors in the pages that follow, I am not that optimistic. I will share credit for any good points they contain. I will, however, share none of the blame for any errors, whether of omission, commission, or judgment, which remain.

Jan P. Vermeer
Lincoln, Nebraska

Chapter One

Studying Local
Newspaper Editorials

Jimmy Carter went to Haiti and to North Korea. Congress considered and rejected health care reform. Bill Clinton's troubles with Whitewater began to emerge. Congress enacted a sweeping crime bill. Republicans offered the nation a "contract" and won the subsequent congressional election. Genocide swept Rwanda, and a peaceful transition to majority rule took place in South Africa. O. J. Simpson and Tonya Harding were accused of crimes that shocked the nation. Protagonists pursued peace in the Middle East and in Bosnia. Welfare reform and gun control were debated in Congress and in the nation at large. It was 1994.

These events generated controversy. Gunboat diplomacy on behalf of democracy in the Caribbean and saber rattling to discourage North Korea from developing nuclear weapons were met with apprehension, and the peaceful resolutions in these instances were greeted with relief. Congressional action or inaction on gun control, welfare reform, crime, and health care frustrated some voters and pleased others; still others simply became angry. The congressional elections in the fall seemed to provide discontented voters with an outlet, and Republicans used that discontent to build support for their platform embodied in the "Contract With America," the centerpiece of their campaign. The tempest that was to become Whitewater began with revelations evoking, at best, a muted response.

U.S. attempts to mediate the civil war in Bosnia worried those people who feared American entanglement in another Vietnam. The Middle East, while offering more hope for peace than in the past, still posed

1

threats of increased terrorism against Americans worldwide. American pride at having assisted, albeit at arm's length, the transition to African National Congress rule in South Africa was tempered by the uncertainty of an appropriate response to the violence in Rwanda.

More typical events also marked 1994. The bureaucracy issued new rules and regulations and enforced existing ones. Congress considered, debated, and passed legislation. The Supreme Court heard oral arguments and issued rulings in a variety of cases. The exceptional may have overshadowed the routine, but the routine persisted.

As a rule, daily newspaper editors across the nation could not and did not ignore national developments in their columns. An editor for the *Jackson (Mississippi) Clarion-Ledger* blamed "special-interest politics, partisan bickering and congressional gridlock"[1] for delays in passing the crime bill. On Bosnia, the editorial writer for the *Fresno (California) Bee* warned that, "The Balkans remain a powder keg," and urged "Washington and Moscow, now the prime outside players . . . [to] quickly find common ground."[2] The Republican victory in the 1994 congressional elections led the *Albuquerque (New Mexico) Journal* to predict either "deep and basic change" or "a promise flameout that will make the first two years of the Clinton presidency look like a triumph."[3] Editors paid attention to the major national and international events of 1994 and made them subjects of their editorials.

National news plays a secondary role, however, to local and state developments in editorials in most of the nation's newspapers. The pattern resembles that for national news generally. Dailies serving small and medium markets concern themselves first with providing news affecting their circulation areas. "Local media flourish," Graber says, "because they concentrate on local events."[4] To the extent they cover national and international developments, dailies rely chiefly on wire services, supplemented by stories bought from stringers and independent news bureaus. Their selection of news stories from wire services and news bureaus reflect local perspectives on the news. As Martin puts it, in the context of national election campaigns, "Local newspapers tend to frame coverage of presidential campaigns in relation to their locality. . . ."[5]

EDITORIALS AND THE NEWS

The interplay of national and local perspectives in newspaper editorials presents the possibility of a range of editorial responses to national affairs. On some issues, virtually every newspaper one might examine would take a position or offer insights; on others, perhaps only a handful or fewer of the nation's daily newspapers may have even bothered to write an editorial. On developments stimulating larger numbers of papers to run editorials, we might find a great deal of similarity or wide contrasts. The more important the local angle to editorial writers, the more contrast among papers one might expect.

Control over content—that is, over the interpretations of the political world citizens encounter—marks a battleground between journalists and political actors. Gadi Wolfsfeld has argued for a theoretical approach that examines the extent to which such control is being exercised (1997), an approach he calls the "political contest model." Using Palestinian–Israeli negotiations as a case study, he discovered that "government's ability to initiate and control events" and "government's ability to regulate the flow of information"[6] influence the extent to which media content reflects governmental objectives, as opposed to the perspectives of political opponents. The more successful government is in controlling events and information, the more the content of the news citizens read and hear will reflect governmental positions. The alternatives matter. Cappella and Jamieson argue that "[w]hen journalists frame political events strategically, they activate existing beliefs and understandings" among readers.[7] By implication, when government officials succeed in framing the news, different "beliefs and understandings" would be activated.

What is deemed newsworthy, ultimately, is a journalistic judgment subject to influence by news sources. The greater the extent to which sources succeed in imposing their perspectives on journalists, the more useful the news will be to achieving their aims. Along these lines, Cook has argued that newsworthiness itself is negotiated between legislator and reporter in the halls of Congress, the premise being that the content of the news story is important to politicians.[8] And I have suggested elsewhere that the issuance of campaign news releases is a prime example of news sources attempting to influence the content of news reports.[9] Although both news sources and journalists strive to present the news as they think appropriate, each operates in conjunction with the other, in a symbiotic fashion.[10]

News is not politically neutral. Two effects are readily discernible. The first, usually characterized as the "agenda-setting" effect, refers to the increased salience of issues widely covered by the media. Members of the public are both more likely to consider an issue important, and to take a position on that issue, when it has received substantial media coverage.[11] More than three decades ago, V. O. Key Jr. asked: "What phases of the political world are reflected in the mirror [of the media]? Which phases are suppressed or ignored?"[12] The answer determines which issues achieve prominence. Widely covered issues result in increased public awareness and increased public pressure on government for action.

The evidence in favor of the agenda-setting notion is not conclusive. It may depend on the issue. When Dalton and his colleagues examined the topic in the light of a presidential election, they noted their belief that "the press is part of the transaction process that sets the agenda of elections, but found . . . little evidence that it predominantly controls agenda setting."[13] But when Jasperson et al. considered both agenda-setting effects and framing effects, they discovered that these factors together "are important pieces of a comprehensive explanation of media influence on aggregate opinion on the budget issue."[14] Because journalists can potentially set the agenda, newsmakers have an incentive to attempt to stimulate increased coverage of some developments and minimal coverage of others.

The second effect concerns the content of the news. The favorability or unfavorability of news content about candidates, government or one of its components, policymakers, or policy advocates affects the public's evaluation of issues on the public agenda. A number of studies have established the variation in tone (e.g., positive or negative content) in news stories.[15] Indeed, for some years, documenting the extent of "bias" or imbalance in news coverage was something of a cottage industry. It has become increasingly clear that variation in tone affects public evaluations as well.[16] Newsmakers, then, also have an incentive to influence the favorability of the coverage they or their pet issues receive. It is not true that it doesn't matter what the press says about you, as long as it spells your name correctly. Just ask Gary Condit.

Control over news may be easier for government and other sources to exert than control over editorials. The White House press operation serves as a case in point. Presidents and their staffs have made the care and feeding of reporters stationed near the Oval Office a fine art.[17] Although journalists have resources of their own to apply, presidents expect to have greater success influencing news content than if they had to encounter the press on reporters' terms. Having media representatives close by also enables presidents to make news on short notice, getting their images and interpretations into the news columns rapidly.

Other newsmakers have more limited abilities to affect news content, but virtually all try to maximize their influence along the way, whether by issuing video or press releases and radio actualities or staging media events.

Editorials, however, are not as apt to be so easily influenced. Although a presidential announcement in the White House press room will most likely result in a news story in most daily newspapers, perhaps even on the front page, it is much less likely that the papers' editors will run an editorial commenting on the president's action. Further, news sources may be able to sway the tone of even putatively objective journalists by selectively providing access to some but not other information. For instance, an interest group may make it easy for a reporter to reach supporters but give no hint as to who might oppose their position. By contrast, however, editorials tend to reflect relatively consistent orientations to political and policy matters. If a paper has editorially opposed public financing of campaigns in the past, it is unlikely to suddenly run an editorial in favor of it simply because some good public relations or news management techniques successfully put a different "spin" on the matter.

A newspaper's editorials provide a vehicle for interpreting the news of the day for its readership, a task editors do not take lightly. By an overwhelming majority, editors surveyed by Hynds, for example, say the editorial page "should provide a forum for the exchange of information and opinion" and "community leadership through stands on issues."[18] "Interpreting the news," however, is a rubric that encompasses a number of elements. Schaefer concisely summarizes them as follows: "[T]raditionally, editorials assess and evaluate policies, politics, and politicians, and . . . provide 'opinion leadership' to the public."[19] Through such assessments, editors can give their readers a framework for understanding political events and criteria for reaching conclusions about them. The point of view editors offer in their editorials comes from the editors' perspectives, outlooks that likely correspond to, and influence, local public discourse.

EDITORIALS AND LOCAL PUBLIC DISCOURSE

Politicians in Washington experience little difficulty in keeping up with the editorial interpretations the national media offer about their actions. They all read or see the *New York Times*, the *Washington Post*, *Newsweek*,

BUT DOES THAT MUTE THE EFFECT?.. PREZ DEBATES?

Time, the major networks, and wire service accounts of breaking news. Further, the editorials published in the major papers provide fodder for conversation, cogitation, and consultation among national political activists. In other words, how these national media report and interpret the news becomes part of public discourse on national political developments in the nation's capital. Inside the Beltway, information and interpretations are important resources, and they help shape the political reality to which national decisionmakers respond.

The coverage and commentary in newspapers published in the many localities across the nation, however, rarely enter public discourse at the national level. To be sure, an occasional article receives national attention, such as the *Miami Herald* story on presidential candidate Gary Hart's affair with Donna Rice, and affects how the nation's political leaders approach a particular problem. And of course, national leaders with local constituencies (e.g., senators and representatives) keep a close ear to editorial commentary in their home bases, as part of their concern with local coverage of their activities.[20] Editorial commentary in local newspapers exists in what one might easily call separate discourse communities, ones that rarely contribute to public discourse at the national level as conducted in Washington.

But local editorials contribute significantly to public discourse in their home communities, in the same ways that editorials in the national media influence public discourse among the nation's policymakers. "The decisions of newspeople," in this case, editorial writers, "are significant, as they fall into systematic patterns that consistently present a particular view of 'reality,'" according to Jamieson and Campbell,[21] a reality within which state and local decisionmakers work. They can, for instance, determine how important the issues they are individually concerned with are, compared to others being discussed and debated. Greater editorial attention to some issues than to others signals policymakers about their relative priority in the eyes of the editors and, by extension, the public. "For many people deeply involved in politics," Herbst points out, "the phenomena of public opinion and mass media are largely conflated."[22]

Because the attentive public can also be assumed to read editorials (Hynds reported in 1984 that 88 percent of editors "believe editorial-page readership is greater [66 percent] or about the same [22 percent]" as ten years earlier),[23] local and state politicians may judge the extent to which their constituents may be concerned with various issues. For example, Herbst quotes one of her respondents, a legislative staffer, as saying that "the editorials in the newspapers will give us some insights on how people out there are thinking about government."[24] Although no research suggests that editorials have a strong agenda-setting effect compared to the effect of straight news, it is not unreasonable to think that editorial emphases on some issues rather than others will influence the policy priorities of both decisionmakers and the attentive public.

When editors in local newspapers choose to devote editorials to national political events and developments, they simultaneously signal the significance of these occurrences for state and local concerns and offer an interpretation of the relationship between state and local issues and the national news. The temptation to connect national events to state and local concerns is strong; when editors draw such connections, the national news becomes relevant not only to national issues but also to state and local controversies. That connection sends a signal about the significance of those affairs. Such a signal is sent even if the editors intend to communicate only that they are leaving commentary on these important issues to the national media. A newspaper that rarely devotes even one editorial to commentary on national or international happenings, such as the *Lansing (Michigan) State Journal*, clearly indicates to its readers that they need concern themselves only with city and state affairs, that news occurring beyond the state's boundaries need not occupy them for long.

As a result, local newspaper commentaries on national news in their editorials contribute to their respective discourse communities, each potentially responding somewhat differently. Because local conditions vary, and because editorials frequently connect local concerns to their interpretations of national news, readers of local editorials in one community are likely to be faced with somewhat different perspectives on the meaning and importance of national and international political developments. Not only are these discourse communities distinct from each other, but also they are all only loosely connected to the discourse community centered on the national media and the nation's political elite.

These local discourse communities are much more difficult for national political leaders to influence. Whereas the president and members of Congress have daily, or almost daily, contact with reporters for the nation's leading media, they have few opportunities to deal with journalists working for the local press, although some presidents have made an effort. Sidney Blumenthal reported on President Clinton's early efforts to reach local media directly, but he pitched it as a means "to go around, manipulate, or control the national press," rather than as a means to influence the content of local news.[25] And, of course, members of Congress are well versed in the care and feeding of the local press,[26] but when they do exert influence, they are more concerned with the presentation of self than with the presentation of issues. As a result, local discourse on national political news is less likely to be swayed by national leaders.

EDITORIALS AND READERS

Locally, editors can reach a sizable readership. A significant proportion of the public receives much of its news from local newspapers. Martin reports that the readership and circulation of local newspapers combined far outpaces the total readership and circulation of the national press, with "elite" newspapers accounting for only 11 percent of daily newspaper circulation in 1994.[27] He adds that "the median newspaper reader is reading a relatively small local paper."[28] Although these figures do not include the audience of the national television networks, through which many people get a lot of their national and international news, television networks offer no direct editorial commentary. The numbers are substantial; many people read local and regional daily newspapers regularly and get quite a bit of their news, even national news, from them.[29]

Readership surveys indicate that editorials are widely read. Bogart reports the results of two surveys. In 1971, "[t]he typical editorial gets exactly the same level of reported readership (25 percent) as the typical newspaper article,"[30] while in 1982, "[t]hirty-five percent of the readers say they try to read editorials 'on a regular basis,' while 43 percent say they 'sometimes glance at them.'"[31] One can safely assume that the more politically active among the citizens would be more likely to be editorial readers than the less active. If so, Bogart's data imply that a very high percentage of politically active people read editorials regularly.

In most areas, the hometown daily newspaper easily outdistances the national dailies in readership. In other words, although the big national newspapers draw large numbers of readers, those readers are scattered across the country, and in any one city (outside the home market for one of the national media, such as Los Angeles, home to the *Los Angeles Times*), more people read the local paper than one of the national papers. In Seattle, for instance, about 20 percent of the population reads a national newspaper, but almost 90 percent reads a metropolitan or local paper, either alone or in combination with a national paper.[32]

HOW LARGE is THAT GROUP

National and local papers do not compete directly. The relationship differs from Rosse's "umbrella model" of competition among newspapers in large metropolitan areas. As Lacy explains it, the major metropolitan daily covers the entire region, and smaller dailies and weeklies cover smaller geographic areas, providing local news and local advertisements.[33] The smaller dailies do not compete directly, because they focus their efforts on separate geographic segments of the metropolitan area; they do, however, compete with the large metropolitan dailies, because they pursue the same readers. However, the national dailies do not compete in that sense. They currently provide so little local or regional news (despite their growing number of regional editions) that the local daily remains the dominant source of news and commentary on state and local affairs for attentive and casual readers alike.

Editors in local daily newspapers, therefore, are likely to be the dominant media voices in their communities. Local television and radio devote very little, if any, of their resources to editorial commentary. Their commentary is sporadic—the audience cannot predict when and where they will encounter a television or radio editorial—and shallow—the topics and stances tend to be noncontroversial and bland. By contrast, newspaper editorials appear daily, consistently in the same place of the paper, cover a wide gamut of subjects from the tame to the inflammatory, and frequently take public officials to task for their decisions. If a local editorial voice is heard, it belongs to the editors of the daily newspaper in the city.

Although these voices speak predominantly of state and local affairs, national and international developments are not ignored. Sometimes a national event simply overpowers other news, reducing state and local concerns to insignificance, almost requiring editorial comment. The surprising outcome of the 1994 congressional elections, or the peaceful resolution of the Haitian crisis with invading U.S. marines already en route clearly falls into this category. At other times, a local connection is so strong that the line between national and local news cannot be clearly drawn. National disputes about tobacco use evoke concerns about the regional economy in North Carolina and Kentucky; editorials quickly follow. And occasionally a hometown personality figures importantly in the news. The investigation into possible corruption involving then–Secretary of Agriculture Mike Espy understandably received much more editorial attention in his home state of Mississippi than elsewhere.

As we will discover in succeeding chapters, editors ran editorials on many other occasions than these. Editorials on national and international affairs were not the rarity one might expect, given the press's expected emphasis on proximity as a news value.[34] Even in the nation's hinterlands, editors offered opinions and insights on national news and international developments.

While no one would argue that editorials appearing in local newspapers play the major role in people's formulation of their opinions, neither should one deny the plausibility of a supporting role for such editorials. While national public opinion is more likely to reflect the influence of the content of the national media, people in various localities will partially formulate their perceptions of national politics on the basis of the content of their local press. Editorials contribute to that perception. To the extent that editors reflect (as well as lead) local public opinion, editorials can give voice to inchoate, not-yet-formed perceptions local residents have. As already noted, Schaefer says editorials "provide 'opinion leadership' to the public."[35] When locally shared values underscore editorial positions, editorials can help citizens form their opinions about national events.[36]

Editorials' effect on citizens, however, forms only part of the picture. State and local policymakers tend to be avid readers of editorials in the local papers, in part because everybody else reads them; decisionmakers have to know what other decisionmakers know and think. As one public official said, "the people who . . . read editorials are very important, and they often wield tremendous influence. The Governor reads the editorial page; so does the Mayor, so do the County Commissioners. And believe me, they respond to what those editorials say."[37]

Local editorials help construct the political reality within which policymakers must act. When editorials bring up national issues and national concerns, state and local policymakers can no longer examine state matters in isolation. Noting how past U.S. Supreme Court cases, for instance, restrict the alternatives available to the state legislature on a problem it is considering makes it more likely that any resulting bill will comply with federal guidelines. By commenting on federal inaction, perhaps, editorials can take the pressure to act off local officials. Editorials about the relevance of national decisions on state and local options thereby introduce national perspectives into local public discourse. The care with which most policymakers at the state and local levels read editorials suggests that these perspectives are at least noticed, probably weighed, and perhaps followed in the decision-making process.

In this way, local newspaper editorials on national and international developments make a difference. These editorials signal readers about the significance of such developments for their lives and their concerns. By making these issues salient to their readership, editorials affect public opinion in their circulation areas, an effect that taken cumulatively can potentially affect national public opinion. These editorials introduce national concerns into state and local decision-making processes by increasing the likelihood that decisionmakers take national factors into account. By injecting such concerns into local public discourse, editorials make it more difficult for officials to consider state and local policy in isolation, as separate from national implications. In sum, these editorials draw connections between national politics on the one hand and local concerns on the other. Because local newspapers serve a distinct market, they target their comments to the unique characteristics of their circulation area. Editorials serve the local audience, even when national topics are the subject, by drawing out their implications for their readers' daily lives.

THE APPROACH OF THIS BOOK

In this book I aim to investigate local editorial commentary on national politics. The assumptions that lie behind this endeavor should, by now, be clear. First, not all the significant commentary on national affairs is published in the nation's elite media. Second, because local commentary can be expected to affect how the attentive public and the political elite in various communities think of national politics, local editorials deserve study. Finally, editorials provide a good avenue for examining commentary because they are almost always locally produced, not subject to the same kind of "spin doctoring" as news reporting is, and indicative of the paper's considered opinion on the topics they address.

Neither communication scholars nor political scientists have devoted much attention to editorials per se. A typical study is one that examines the effect of editorial endorsements on election outcomes.[38] These studies generally find an impact, although limited in magnitude. A case in point: Dalton, Beck, and Huckfeldt find that "the content of editorials directly influenced candidate preferences . . . [b]ut the effect was modest."[39] Ernest Hynds has conducted periodic surveys of editors to discover their perceptions of editorials, their role, and their future.[40] Others have looked at editorials in locally or chain-owned newspapers to see if ownership made a difference.[41] David Myers is one of the few who have spent much effort on the content of editorials, but he has limited himself to the issues raised during election campaigns.[42]

More recently, political scientists have begun to use the content of editorials as a way to address other important questions. Segal and Cover, for instance, use editorial evaluations of Supreme Court nominees as an independent antecedent measure of the nominees' ideology,[43] and more recently to estimate the salience of court cases as a way to predict Supreme Court action.[44] Dragoo and her colleagues used editorials to examine responses to Supreme Court decisions on freedom of religion cases.[45] Entman studied the effects of editorials on people with liberal, conservative, and moderate leanings, finding that editorials influence people's opinions subtly but significantly.[46] Gonzalez's research on expectations about presidents relies on editorials, arguing that "these expectations are at least in part formed and reflected in editorials."[47] Schaefer actually tries to explain the content of editorials, specifically those commenting on presidential State of the Union messages, finding that the political context affects the favorability of editorial assessments of State of the Union speeches.[48]

As a rule, these studies have generally relied chiefly either on editorials in the nation's elite media[49] or on editorials from a variety of papers on a limited subject.[50] Useful as the insights such research can generate are, they provide us with little understanding of patterns of editorial commentary in local papers across the nation and on a wide range of topics. No wide ranging study of editorial content in local papers has previously been conducted.

Nevertheless, research on local papers and their content is also needed. Public discourse on national politics takes place outside the Beltway as well as within, and the content of that discourse influences how citizens and policymakers alike across the country perceive national political institutions and respond to them. Naturally, the actual actions taken by Congress, the president, and the Supreme Court affect the conditions under which people live and state and local policy decisions are made, but citizens' and leaders' perceptions also help determine their responses to the exigencies of the day. Whether in debates on the floor of the state legislature, discussion among citizens at a neighborhood gathering, or an argument carried out through letters-to-the-editor, public discourse helps structure the decision-making process used by both voters and policymakers. How the actions of the national government are depicted and interpreted for them provides the context for political responses.

Typically, one interested in public discourse on national political institutions and processes would study the news coverage the institutions
receive[51] or the responses of the public to political events, such as
through public opinion polls or voting.[52] Research of this sort begins
and ends with a national perspective, implicitly assuming political information is relatively uniformly available everywhere. Perhaps as far
as exposure to television network newscasts and to newsmagazines is
concerned, that assumption need not be questioned, although clearly
the information environments within which people live differ greatly.[53]
But these studies do not examine the way news coverage of political
developments enters into public discourse in states and localities, and
because the focus tends to be national, they leave little room for the significant variation in media environments across the nation.

The extent and import of that variation are considerable. Delli Carpini
and Keeter take issue with the assumption that "adequate information is
available through the modern news media, regardless of where an individual lives," for the acquisition of political knowledge.[54] They conclude
that "the relation between availability of information and citizen knowledge levels is so strong in certain situations that the nature of the information environment is the most important predictor of knowledge."[55]

My contention is that newspaper editorials play a major role in bringing national political developments to bear on the public discourse in
the area the paper serves, calling readers' attention to events and decisions in Washington, D.C. (and elsewhere in the nation), that potentially affect state and local concerns. Because editors consciously attempt to interpret the news, consciously address policymakers, and
consciously highlight noteworthy developments by devoting editorials
to them, editorials are a significant link between national political developments and state and local public discourse on them.

Local media are logistically difficult to study. Few have attempted a
wide analysis. Just, Crigler, and colleagues collaborated, each responsible for collecting media reports on an election they studied in one of
four geographic areas.[56] Schaefer used *Editorials on File* to construct
a national sample of newspaper editorials.[57] Martin compared two local dailies with two national dailies.[58] Kaniss's ambitious study centered chiefly on Philadelphia, with extensive evidence from three other
cities.[59] Nevertheless, despite the difficulties, local news is important,
mostly because the local newspapers do more to structure the information context for citizens than do the national media. They do more
because they can relate the news to local matters about which citizens

are likely to care. Because they survive on the patronage of local readers, newspapers must make their coverage and commentary relevant to
them. Mondak noted that "the local newspaper plays a crucial role in
enabling citizens to appreciate the local importance of national politics."[60] "All politics is local," Tip O'Neill was wont to say; "most news
is local," would be an accurate corollary. Even national news is local:
Martin finds that "local newspapers tend to frame coverage of presidential campaigns in relation to their locality."[61] Only by examining
local newspapers can we get a more complete picture of news coverage as citizens experience it.

This study is based on an examination of all the editorials published
in 1994 in ten medium-sized daily newspapers from across the nation.
The cities where these papers are published represent all regions of the
continental United States. These cities range in size from Albuquerque,
New Mexico (411,994) to Albany, New York (100,031). Seven are
state capitals (all except Fresno, California; Albuquerque, New Mexico; and Lexington, Kentucky). In some cases, the cities are located
some distance away from a larger metropolitan area dominated by big
city newspapers: Boise, Idaho; Jackson, Mississippi; and Raleigh,
North Carolina, are examples. Others fall within the reach of a major
media market, such as Lansing, Michigan, near Detroit; Providence,
Rhode Island, near Boston; and Albany, New York, near New York
City. They range in circulation from 39,421 (the *Lincoln [Nebraska]
Journal*) to 197,120 (the *Providence [Rhode Island] Journal*). The city
in question is in every case either the center of a separately defined
Standard Statistical Metropolitan Area (nine cities) or the capital and
largest city of a state (Providence).

A year such as 1994 serves as an excellent time period for a study
of this nature. News coverage and editorial commentary were not
skewed by the weight of a presidential election, leaving more room
for editors to engage a wider range of subjects. At the same time, congressional elections presented editors an opportunity to evaluate what
local representatives had accomplished in Washington. No one foreign policy issue dominated the public agenda; one need only note, by
contrast, the extent to which the Gulf War and the fighting in
Afghanistan overwhelmed other news subjects. Significantly, too,
1994 saw the retirement of a Supreme Court justice and the naming
of his replacement, a relatively rare occurrence that gives editors an
occasion to peek behind the veil shielding the Court from public view.
One should also point out the major issues with which Congress grap-

Table 1.1: Newspapers and Circulations in Study

Newspaper	Circulation	
Albany Times Union	101,017	*N F*
Albuquerque Journal	117,932	*S W*
Boise Idaho Statesman	64,435	*W*
Fresno Bee	152,572	*W*
Jackson Clarion-Ledger	111,794	*S*
Lansing State Journal	71,261	*MW*
Lexington Herald Leader	84,890	*S*
Lincoln Journal	39,421	*MW*
Providence Journal	197,120	*NY*
Raleigh News & Observer	150,738	*SE*

Source: Circulation figures are from *Gale's Directory of Publications and Broadcast Media* (Detroit: Gale Research, Inc., 1995), various pages.

pled in 1994: both the crime bill and the Clinton health-care proposal not only grabbed public attention but also raised issues salient to local readers.

It is likely that almost any year chosen for this study would have yielded similarly striking events. The point is, however, that the events of 1994 were striking enough for one to expect local newspaper editors to address them in their editorials, but not so exceptional that the patterns found there would fit only 1994. Therefore, even though the newspapers used here do not represent a randomly drawn sample, and even though 1994 is only one year, I am quite confident that editorial commentary examined here yields insights that we can trust.[62]

The method is unabashedly qualitative, with the exception of some of the work reported in chapter 2. My intent here is not to test hypotheses but to discover what the editors said and how they said it. Others may prefer a different approach to these editorials. I would hope that the conclusions, however, would be similar.

THE REST OF THE BOOK

Chapter 2 examines these editorials as a whole. I consider variations in the numbers of editorials published by these newspapers and in the topics they

address. Briefly, and unsurprisingly, the larger the newspaper, the greater
the number of editorials published. Two competing considerations for
topic choice, audience concerns, and newsworthiness help account for the
distribution of editorials among the various topics they deal with. Chapter
3 focuses on editorials discussing Congress and the local members of
Congress. Specifically, this chapter explores the contribution editorial
commentary makes to public assessments of members of Congress and of
the institution itself. It concludes that, despite the sharp criticism to which
editors subject Congress and its members, an underlying respect for the
body survives.

Chapter 4 subjects the editorials on the presidency to the same
treatment. The prominence given the president in the news columns,
so often noted by media scholars, is paralleled by the emphasis given
him by editorials, as well. These editorials show the president as the
chief representative of the nation as a whole in international affairs,
but as a less dominant actor in domestic matters, while Congress is
depicted as playing a distinctly second-string role. The bureaucracy
and federal policy administration are also frequently the targets of editorial commentary. The nature of that commentary is explored in
chapter 5, with an emphasis on the explanation for the decisions the
bureaucracy makes. It will be discovered that the bureaucracy has few
fans among editors, and that the bureaucracy is the topic chiefly when
a problem arises.

Chapter 6 is devoted to editorials on the U.S. Supreme Court. The
findings suggest that editors are relatively respectful of the Court, accepting its decisions with little dissent. Editors do not, contrary to my
expectations, explain Court results and individual Justices' voting by
using ideological labels. The frequency with which editors cite past
Court decisions in discussions of current policy considerations is new
and interesting evidence for an impact of the Supreme Court that traditional studies of the Court's impact have not found.

Chapter 7 explores the connections these editorials draw between national matters on the one hand and state and local concerns on the other.
Although previous chapters will have presented many specific examples of such connections, in this chapter, I find that editors adopt what
some have called "pragmatic federalism"[63] as their approach to national
and state relationships. The final chapter presents concluding remarks
on the perspective on national politics citizens get from these local
newspaper editorials.

NOTES

1. "Crime Bill: Criminals Have a Lot of Allies in Crime," *Jackson (Mississippi) Clarion-Ledger*, 13 August 1994, 12(A).

2. "Groping for Bosnian Peace," *Fresno (California) Bee*, 25 February 1994, 6(B).

3. "American Voters Chose GOP Plan for Future," *Albuquerque (New Mexico) Journal*, 13 November 1994, 2(B).

4. Doris Graber, *Mass Media and American Politics*, 5th ed. (Washington, D.C.: Congressional Quarterly, 1997), 107.

5. Paul Martin, "Over the Wire and Then What?" (paper presented at the annual meeting of the Midwest Political Science Association, Chicago, Ill., April 1996), 3.

6. Gadi Wolfsfeld, "Fair Weather Friends: The Varying Role of the News Media in the Arab-Israeli Peace Process," *Political Communication* 14, no. 1 (January/March 1997): 31–32.

7. Joseph N. Cappella and Kathleen Hall Jamieson, *Spiral of Cynicism: The Press and the Public Good* (New York: Oxford University Press, 1997), 208.

8. Timothy Cook, *Making Laws & Making News: Media Strategies in the U.S. House of Representatives* (Washington, D.C.: Brookings Institution, 1989).

9. Jan Pons Vermeer, *"For Immediate Release:" Candidate Press Releases in American Political Campaigns* (Westport, Conn.: Greenwood Press, 1982).

10. See Michael Baruch Grossman and Martha Joynt Kumar, *Portraying the President: The White House and the News Media* (Baltimore, Md.: Johns Hopkins University Press, 1981), on how presidential relationships with the press can be understood in terms of cooperation and conflict.

11. See, among others, Maxwell E. McCombs and Donald L. Shaw, "The Agenda-Setting Function of Mass Media," *Public Opinion Quarterly* 36 (summer 1972): 176–87; and Lutz Erbring, Edie N. Goldenberg, and Arthur H. Miller, "Front-Page News and Real-World Cues: A New Look at Agenda-Setting by the Media," *American Journal of Political Science* 24 (February 1980): 16–49.

12. V. O. Key Jr. *Public Opinion and American Democracy* (New York: Alfred A. Knopf, 1961), 390.

13. Russell J. Dalton, Paul Allen Beck, Robert Huckfeldt, and William Koetzle, "A Test of Media-Centered Agenda Setting: Newspaper Content and Public Interests in a Presidential Election," *Political Communication* 15 (October/December 1998): 476.

14. Amy E. Jasperson, Dhavan V. Shah, Mark Watts, Ronald J. Faber, and David P. Fan, "Framing and the Public Agenda: Media Effects on the Importance of the Federal Budget Deficit," *Political Communication* 15 (April/June 1998), 219.

15. Frederick T. Smoller, *The Six O'Clock Presidency: A Theory of Presidential Press Relations in the Age of Television* (New York: Praeger, 1990);

Michael J. Robinson and Margaret A. Sheehan, *Over the Wire and On TV: CBS and UPI in Campaign '80* (New York: Russell Sage Foundation, 1983); Wolfsfeld, "Fair Weather Friends."

16. David P. Fan, *Predictions of Public Opinion from the Mass Media* (Westport, Conn.: Greenwood Press, 1988); Thomas E. Mann and Norman J. Ornstein, eds., *Congress, the Press, and the Public* (Washington, D.C.: American Enterprise Institute and Brookings Institution, 1994); Silvo Lenart, *Shaping Political Attitudes: The Impact of Interpersonal Communication and Mass Media* (Thousand Oaks, Calif.: Sage Publications, 1994).

17. Grossman and Kumar, *Portraying the President.*

18. Ernest Hynds, "Editorials, Opinion Pages Still Have Vital Roles at Most Newspapers," *Journalism Quarterly* 61, no. 3 (autumn 1984): 635.

19. Todd M. Schaefer, "Persuading the Persuaders: Presidential Speeches and Editorial Opinion," *Political Communication* 14 (January/March 1997): 98.

20. Michael J. Robinson, "Three Faces of Congressional Media," in *the New Congress*, eds. Thomas E. Mann and Norman J. Ornstein (Washington, D.C.: American Enterprise Institute, 1981), 55–96.

21. Kathleen Hall Jamieson and Karlyn Kohrs Campbell, *The Interplay of Influence: Mass Media & Their Publics in News, Advertising, Politics* (Belmont, Calif.: Wadsworth, 1983), 2.

22. Susan Herbst, *Reading Public Opinion: How Political Actors View the Democratic Process* (Chicago: University of Chicago Press, 1998), 5.

23. Hynds, "Editorials, Opinion Pages," 635.

24. Herbst, *Reading Public Opinion*, 67.

25. Sidney Blumenthal, "Letter from Washington: The Syndicated Presidency," *New Yorker*, 5 April 1993, 46.

26. See, for instance, the examples in Ronald E. Elving, "Brighter Lights, Wider Windows: Presenting Congress in the 1990s," in Mann and Ornstein, eds, *Congress, the Press, and the Public*, 171–206, esp. 181–82.

27. Martin, "Over the Wire," 3.

28. Martin, "Over the Wire," 4.

29. In Alabama, a survey reported that almost 57 percent of respondents agree that their local paper keeps them adequately informed on national news. I thank Samuel H. Fisher, University of South Alabama, for providing me with these results from the USA Polling Group survey of 425 Alabama residents from July 12 through July 15, 1993. The margin of error for the sample was plus or minus 5 percent, with a confidence level of 95 percent.

30. Leo Bogart, *Press and Public: Who Reads What, When, Where, and Why in American Newspapers*, 2nd ed. (Hillsdale, N.J.: Lawrence Erlbaum, 1989), 177.

31. Bogart, *Press and Public*, 178.

32. Michelle Johnson, Keith Stamm, Joanne Lisosky, and Jeanette James, "Differences among Newspapers in Contributions to Knowledge of National Public Affairs," *Newspaper Research Journal* 13, no. 3 (summer 1995): 88.

33. Stephen Lacy, "Competition among Metropolitan Daily, Small Daily and Weekly Newspapers," *Journalism Quarterly* 61, no. 3 (autumn 1984): 640–44, 742.

34. Graber, *Mass Media and American Politics*, 107–8.

35. Schaefer, "Persuading the Persuaders," 98.

36. The argument here is analogous to that which Richard Funston makes about the U.S. Supreme Court. See Richard Funston, *A Vital National Seminar: The Supreme Court in American Political Life* (Palo Alto, Calif.: Mayfield, 1978).

37. Quoted in Phyllis Kaniss, *Making Local News* (Chicago: University of Chicago Press, 1991), 162.

38. See, among others, James E. Gregg, "Newspaper Editorial Endorsements and California Elections," *Journalism Quarterly* 42, no. 3 (autumn 1964): 532–38; Robert S. Erikson, "The Influence of Newspaper Endorsements in Presidential Elections," *American Journal of Political Science* 20, no. 2 (May 1976): 207–33; Robert E. Hurd and Michael W. Singletary, "Newspaper Influence on the 1980 Presidential Election Vote," *Journalism Quarterly* 61, no. 2 (summer 1985): 332–38; Byron St. Dizier, "The Effect of Newspaper Endorsements and Party Identification on Voting Choice," *Journalism Quarterly* 62, no. 3 (autumn 1985): 589–94.

39. Russell J. Dalton, Paul A. Beck, and Robert Huckfeldt, "Partisan Cues and the Media: Information Flows in the 1992 Presidential Election," *American Political Science Review* 92 (March 1998): 125.

40. Ernest C. Hynds, "Editorial Pages Are Taking Stands, Providing Forums," *Journalism Quarterly* 53, no. 3 (autumn 1976): 532–35; Ernest C. Hynds and Charles H. Martin, "Editorial Writers Tell How They Go About Their Work," *Journalism Quarterly* 54, no. 4 (winter 1978): 776–79; Hynds, "Editorials, Opinion Pages;" Ernest Hynds and Erika Archibald, "Improved Editorial Pages Can Help Papers' Communities," *Newspaper Research Journal* 17, no. 1-2 (winter/spring 1996): 14–24.

41. David Demers, "Corporate Newspaper Structure, Editorial Page Vigor, and Social Change," *Journalism and Mass Communication Quarterly* 73, no. 4 (winter 1996): 857–77. See also the literature he cites.

42. David S. Myers, "Editorials and Foreign Affairs in Recent Presidential Campaigns," *Journalism Quarterly* 59, no. 4 (winter 1982): 541–47.

43. Jeffrey A. Segal and Albert D. Cover, "Ideological Values and the Votes of U.S. Supreme Court Justices," *American Political Science Review* 83, no. 2 (June 1989): 557–66.

44. Lee Epstein and Jeffrey A. Segal, "Measuring Issue Salience," *American Journal of Political Science* 44 (January 2000), 66–83.

45. Kathleen Dragoo, Melissa Duits, and William Haltom, "Reconsidering the Nagel-Erikson Hypothesis: Editorial Reactions to Church-State Cases," *American Politics Quarterly* 21, no. 3 (June 1993): 368–78.

46. Robert M. Entman, *Democracy Without Citizens: Media and the Decay of American Politics* (New York: Oxford University Press, 1989), 75–88.

47. Noelle Gonzalez, "Editorials and Evaluations of Presidents: Public Expectations of Incumbent Presidents and Retrospective Voting" (paper presented at the annual meeting of the Midwest Political Science Association, Chicago, Ill., April 1994), 5.

48. Schaefer, "Persuading the Persuaders."

49. Myers, "Editorials and Foreign Affairs."

50. Dragoo, Duits, and Haltom, "Reconsidering the Nagel-Erikson Hypothesis"; Schaefer, "Persuading the Persuaders."

51. Cook, *Making Laws & Making News*; Richard Davis, *Decisions and Images: The Supreme Court and the Press* (Englewood Cliffs, N.J.: Prentice-Hall, 1994); Grossman and Kumar, *Portraying the President*.

52. See, for instance, John Zaller, *The Nature and Origins of Mass Opinion* (New York: Cambridge University Press, 1992).

53. For example, Edie N. Goldenberg and Michael W. Traugott, "Mass Media Effects on Recognizing and Rating Candidates in U.S. Senate Elections," in *Campaigns in the News: Mass Media and Congressional Elections*, ed. Jan Pons Vermeer (Westport, Conn.: Greenwood Press, 1987), 109–31.

54. Michael X. Delli Carpini and Scott Keeter, *What Americans Know About Politics and Why It Matters* (New Haven, Conn.: Yale University Press, 1996), 210.

55. Delli Carpini and Keeter, *What Americans Know*, 271–72.

56. Marion R. Just, Ann N. Crigler, Dean E. Alger, Timothy E. Cook, Montague Kern, and Darrell M. West, *Crosstalk: Citizens, Candidates, and the Media in a Presidential Campaign* (Chicago: University of Chicago Press, 1996).

57. Schaefer, "Persuading the Persuaders."

58. Martin, "Over the Wire."

59. Kaniss, *Making Local News*.

60. Jeffery J. Mondak, *Nothing to Read: Newspapers and Elections in a Social Experiment* (Ann Arbor: University of Michigan Press, 1995), 143.

61. Martin, "Over the Wire," 3.

62. Having said this, I must also add that the choice of 1994 was also quite natural for me, the idea for this book coming to me in the spring of 1995. The year just ended seemed to be the best time period to study.

63. Parris N. Glendening and Mavis Mann Reeves, *Pragmatic Federalism: An Intergovernmental View of American Government* (Pacific Palisades, Calif.: Palisades Publishing, 1977).

Chapter Two

Uniformity and Diversity
in Topic Selection

On Sunday, September 18, 1994, President Bill Clinton announced that an agreement had been reached with the military junta, led by General Raoul Cedras, governing Haiti. Cedras and his colleagues would resign and leave Haiti by October 15 of that year, thereby making unnecessary an invasion by U.S. Marines to restore democracy in Haiti and Jean-Bertrand Ariste to the presidency. The agreement was forged in face-to-face discussions between members of the junta and former president Jimmy Carter, Senator Sam Nunn, and retired General Colin Powell while Marines were already en route to Haiti. The nation breathed a collective sigh of relief.

By Tuesday morning, September 20, nine of the ten newspapers included in this study had run an editorial expressing their relief that the planned invasion was averted at the last moment. Only the *Lansing State Journal* ignored the event editorially. But editors at the other nine newspapers thought the news worthy of comment. The importance of the issues, the drama and conflict involved, and the participation of Clinton, Carter, and Powell all helped make the event irresistible. Not that they all agreed: the *Albany Times-Union* could not "see the sense of risking American and Haitian lives" with little hope of real democracy taking root in Haiti.[1] But the *Raleigh News and Observer* called it "a triumph for freedom" and criticized "congressional naysayers" who had opposed the show of force that led to the agreement as a "hypocritical bunch."[2] The consensus, however, was that Carter and Clinton deserved credit for advancing the cause of democracy in Haiti without having to use military force.

Not every development merits editorial commentary in most newspapers. When an American Eagle commuter plane crashed near the Raleigh-Durham airport in North Carolina on December 13, 1994, killing fifteen people, only two of these ten newspapers found it worth editorial space. Predictably, one was the *Raleigh News and Observer*, for whom the crash was local news, too. Its editorial focused on the need for federal regulation; the local event presented an opportunity to talk about national aviation safety.[3] The other editorial appeared in the *Providence Journal*; it, too, focused on a national issue: government regulation of civilian air travel. Accidents such as this one, the editors suggest, "ought to force consideration of whether deregulation has, on the whole, been worth it."[4] (At the end of its editorial, however, the *Journal* voiced its sympathy for survivors of the victims, listing two local residents who died in the crash. This paper, too, found a local link to the news.)

National and international news does not automatically become fodder for editorial writers at daily newspapers that serve a local or regional market. A great deal of variability marks the choices editors make. The extent of that variation and some explanations for the pattern of topic selection is the subject of this chapter.

TWO SOURCES OF EDITORIAL TOPICS

The nature of the commentary daily newspaper editors throughout the nation make on national political events and institutions reflects two basic motives: editors' desire to comment on the events of the day (the "news," so to speak) and their desire to please the local audience that they seek to address. If the events of the times were to determine the topics editors choose for their themes, there would be virtually no variation from newspaper to newspaper. If, on the other hand, editors respond to local readers' assumed concerns when they devote their editorials to some national political events and developments, there would be much less, perhaps only minimal, similarity among newspapers in their selection of editorial subjects.

Under canons of objectivity which guide contemporary journalists, the news columns inform the public of developments and occurrences that warrant reporting, while the editorial pages give editors and others an opportunity to comment on, to evaluate, to respond to, or to analyze these events.[5] If an occurrence embodies more of the characteristics that journalists think indicate newsworthiness, such as timeliness, involvement of VIPs, unexpectedness, and conflict,[6] it is more likely to be reported as news, and more newspapers are likely to report it. Because reporters share perceptions of newsworthiness, one can expect them to make similar decisions, whether they report the news in Arizona or Vermont. It is not surprising that "a remarkable standardization of news content across various media outlets" results.[7] Under objectivity, newsworthiness, not a reporter's biases, determines what will appear in the paper.

These constraints do not limit editorial topic selection. Significant as well as insignificant news stories may become the subjects of editorials. In fact, a newspaper's editorials may even address developments so minor that they warrant either little or no space in the news columns. No standards of "newsworthiness" dictate editorial content.

Because there is a great deal more space available for "straight news" reporting in newspapers, many more events can be brought to readers' attention in the news than in the papers' editorials. Selection of topics for editorials is therefore potentially more difficult; rarely can a paper's editors write on more than four topics on any one day, and few daily newspapers run even that many editorials every day. Whereas news stories not compelling enough to rate a front page position can be published on the inside pages of the paper, editors have no consolation prize to award to editorials for which the paper has no space. There is no implicit expectation that editorial topics should faithfully mirror news coverage. Bennett suggests, however, that "news professionals . . . tend to 'index' the range of voices and viewpoints in both news and editorials according to the range of views expressed in mainstream government debate about a given topic.[8]

Although the choice of subjects is more difficult, editors have fewer standards to guide their selection. Newsworthiness criteria compel coverage of many events, and wire services make the decisions that provide much of the national news local dailies have available.[9] But editors can choose to comment on a front-page news story or leave it alone. They can decide to chastise or to praise national officials for a dramatic action that the news columns reported. They can emphasize a series of investigative reports with editorial comment or let the findings speak for themselves. Decisions about news are, one might say, a conditioned response to stimuli; editorial decisions are not so conditioned.

But, what does that tell us about patterns?

Editorials need not address earth-shaking issues. There, editors can indulge their impulses, if they wish. They can repeatedly address a pet issue; they can write about a minor event that, for them, epitomizes human wisdom or folly; they can ask aloud why nothing has been done on a long-forgotten concern. Editorials can reflect idiosyncratic concerns, whether the editor's or the locality's. One would therefore expect more variation in editorial topics among newspapers than in news content.

Because editorial space is more limited, editors' choices of topics signal their perception of the importance of the issue being addressed, much as the selection of some stories to appear on the front page alerts readers to the importance of those developments. Walter Lippmann long ago alerted us to the significance of such signaling by journalists. "The press is like the beam of a searchlight that moves restlessly about, bringing one episode and then another out of the darkness into vision."[10] Following Lasswell, Graber refers to the media's surveillance function, which "throws the spotlight of publicity on selected people, organizations, and events."[11] Editorials operate in conjunction with news reports to indicate to the public what of importance is occurring in their world, and equally importantly, how the events of the day relate to the issues with which the editors think the public ought to concern itself. When editors choose to comment on one topic rather than another, then, they distinctly indicate the importance they ascribe to it. Such a clear signal is hard for a reader of editorials to miss.

Given the range of options editors have in selecting topics for their editorials, and given the discretion they have in making that selection, not to mention the difference among newspapers' market areas and their correspondingly different concerns and interests, a wide variation in editorial topics in papers across the nation could be expected. But as journalists, editors can also be expected to make similar judgments about the newsworthiness of various developments and therefore to reach similar conclusions about topics worthy of editorial comment. An earlier study compared topic selection between two newspapers in the same city, therefore presumably addressing much the same audience, and found that while a great deal of diversity in topic selection occurred, there was also substantial overlap. The more newsworthy the subject matter, the more likely that editors in both papers would address the topic.[12]

If one looks at the entire range of issues addressed by newspaper editors in their editorial columns, of course, one would chiefly see diversity of topics. Each paper can be expected to focus substantial attention on local and state issues, and these by definition vary from locale to locale. But national events are presumably equally newsworthy across the nation. (I disregard here, for the moment, the fact that many national developments take place in some particular location, where the news would be as much local as it is national.) That would make the topics equally attractive for comment everywhere in the country, and editors could be expected to respond similarly regardless of location.

To the extent that news characteristics dominate editors' selection criteria, one would expect a great deal of uniformity. To the extent that editors across the nation recognize the significance of an action by Congress, a statement by the president, or a decision by the Supreme Court, one would expect that editors of dailies in every section of the nation would reach similar conclusions about whether to devote editorial space and time to commenting on it. Some such developments are likely to be seen as so significant that editors virtually everywhere will decide they should say something about them in their editorials. Others are less likely to be perceived as that important, and so a lower proportion of editors would choose to comment, while the remaining national news is not likely to warrant much commentary in local newspaper editorials at all. Editorial commentary guided by decisions about the significance of the events under discussion I call "news-driven."

On the other hand, however, an editor would want to address readers with commentary they are likely to perceive as relevant to their concerns. If readers do not consider the topic worth their consideration, they are more likely to skip reading the editorial completely. So editors have an incentive to limit their selection to the issues their readers will find worthwhile. Because issues of concern to readers vary with factors unique to each paper's market area, we would expect a corresponding diversity in editors' selection of editorial topics. I call editorial commentary guided by decisions about appeal to the readership "audience-driven."

If editorials in newspapers across the country deal with similar issues at similar times, people in all sections of the nation will be exposed to the same topics, even though the slant of the commentary may differ significantly. If editorials, however, do not treat similar issues, people living in different areas will be exposed to much different pictures of what is important. In other words, the signals, sent by editors about which national events and developments are worth attending to may be quite different. The development of a national political agenda and the extent to which U.S. residents across the nation see themselves faced with similar issues may be affected. In other words, the more news-driven editorial topic selection is, the more uniform citizens' pictures of the nation and its concerns will be, regardless of their place of residence; but the more audience-driven that topic selection is, the more disparate that picture may be.

Using this study's medium-sized daily newspapers to examine the impact of these two factors works well. Large dailies would not provide appropriate evidence, because editors at those papers see themselves as addressing at least a regional if not a national audience. The disparity between news-driven and audience-driven topic selection would be a great deal less, because what is newsworthy among national events and developments is also of interest to national audiences. But one can expect more disparity between news-driven and audience-driven concerns in editorials from medium-sized dailies.

As noted in the previous chapter, the circulation of the papers in this study ranged from just under 40,000 for the *Lincoln Journal* to just under 200,000 for the *Providence Journal*. Half the newspapers had a circulation between 70,000 and 120,000. The mean circulation was 109,118, with a sizable standard deviation of 45,155. Because circulation means revenue, and therefore different levels of resources, this range of size will allow us to assess the effect of circulation on editorial topic selection. The market for each of these papers is also well defined. The city in question is in every case either the center of a separately defined Standard Statistical Metropolitan Area (nine cities) or the capital and largest city of a state (Providence).

Table 2.1 reports the total editorials each newspaper published in 1994, along with its circulation. The *Fresno Bee* published almost twice as many editorials (1,048) as the *Lexington Herald-Leader* (550), but most papers ran between 650 and 850 editorials. Because virtually every issue of every newspaper included at least one editorial, and in most cases two or three, not much variation in the total number should be expected. The data set then includes just over two editorials per paper per day.

I coded each editorial as to whether it dealt with a national or international issue, whether it referred to a national institution (the president, Congress or one of its members, a federal agency, or the Supreme Court), and whether it drew a connection between the de-

Table 2.1: Circulation, Total Editorials, and Editorials on National and International Issues for Ten Daily Newspapers, 1994.

Newspaper	Circulation	Total Editorials	Editorials on National Issues	Editorials on International Issues
Boise Idaho Statesman	64,435	778	133	37
Providence Journal	197,120	845	241	145
Lansing State Journal	71,261	689	61	1
Jackson Clarion-Ledger	111,794	973	206	59
Lincoln Journal	39,421	681	160	22
Fresno Bee	152,572	1,048	288	169
Raleigh News and Observer	150,738	906	177	20
Lexington Herald-Leader	84,890	550	90	5
Albuquerque Journal	117,932	678	172	63
Albany Times-Union	101,017	675	192	80

Source: Circulation figures are from *Gale's Directory of Publications and Broadcast Media,* Detroit, Michigan: Gale Research, Inc., 1995 edition. Data on editorials computed by author.

velopment presented in the editorial and a local concern or person. In addition, the national issue addressed in the editorial was also identified.

I expect that circulation, as a surrogate for available resources, would be related to the extent that national and international issues are addressed in the paper's editorials. I also expect to find that smaller papers are more likely to draw connections between the locality and the topic under discussion. Finally, I expect to find that the more "important" the story, the more likely that more of these newspapers would choose to devote one or more editorials to it. The "importance" of the news is indicated by its appearance the various wire services' lists of the top ten news stories of 1994. If a newspaper writes more editorials on these issues, its topic selection is more likely to be news-driven. If its editorials on national and international issues are more likely to draw connections to state and local concerns, then its topic selection is more likely to be audience-driven.

FINDINGS

Editorials on National and International Matters

These daily newspapers published significantly different numbers of editorials that dealt with national or international affairs. The *Fresno Bee* ran 457 such editorials over the course of the year, more than one per day on average, while the *Lansing State Journal* editors wrote only 62, just over one per week. Most papers ran between 170 and 275 editorials that dealt at least in part with national and international affairs. Put differently, almost half the *Bee*'s editorials concerned national or international news, while less than 10 percent of the *State Journal*'s editorials did. Lansing and Fresno residents were sent much different signals about the relevance of affairs of the nation and of the world. The grand total of such editorials in all ten papers combined was 2,321.

There is much less variation among the newspapers in the number of editorials dealing exclusively with state and local affairs. While the *Fresno Bee* published almost five times as many national and international editorials than the *Lansing State Journal*, the paper with the most state and local editorials, the *Raleigh News and Observer*, had less than twice such editorials than the paper with the least, the *Albany Times-Union* (708 to 403). Each paper, therefore, had plenty to say, but some say more editorially about national and international affairs than others.

There is a sizable, but not an overwhelming, relationship between a paper's circulation and the number of editorials referring to nonlocal events and institutions. The simple correlation is .61, suggesting that just over 36 percent of the variance in the number of such editorials is accounted for by differences in circulation. If we standardize the measure of nonlocal editorials by dividing it by the number of total editorials published in the newspaper that year, the correlation is smaller ($r = .49$), with just a quarter of the variance explained. Nevertheless, the relationship persists, so that we can conclude that larger papers are (1) more likely to devote editorials to discussions of national and international affairs, and (2) more likely to devote a greater proportion of their editorials to such topics.

Similar conclusions can be drawn from examining the relationship between circulation and editorials on national and on international topics separately. In both cases, the correlation coefficient is just about .70. But, interestingly, the correlation coefficients for the relationships between a paper's circulation and the percentage of its editorials that deal with national and with international subjects respectively are quite different. The circulation/percent national correlation is .53, but for the percentage of international issues, it is .70. Larger papers are more likely to run editorials on national and on international topics, but larger papers are much more likely to devote a larger proportion of their total editorials to international affairs.

Of the national institutions, the Congress, the president, the bureaucracy, and the Supreme Court, editorials were more likely to mention the president (749 editorials) and Congress or one of its members (661). The bureaucracy was discussed in 402 separate editorials, with the Court involved in 159. These numbers are not surprising, especially when we recognize that members of Congress are also local news on many occasions. When we separate editorials dealing with national affairs from those dealing with international matters, a different pattern emerges. Congress is the main institution in only sixteen editorials on international affairs, compared with the president's 292. But nationally focused editorials are more likely to deal with Congress or one of its members than the president, 529 to 426. These editorials clearly reflect the president's dominant role in foreign affairs and Congress's preoccupation with domestic policies.

This aggregate pattern, however, is chiefly the product of differences in circulation. Editorials referring to Congress or one of its members are just as likely to appear in smaller as in larger papers; the correlation between the percent of congressional editorials and circulation is virtually zero: -.01. However, the correlation between the percent of presidential editorials and circulation is sizable and positive: .60. Because larger papers are more likely to run editorials on international affairs, and since those editorials are more likely to deal with the president than with Congress, circulation and presidential editorials are correlated. But because Congress and its members come up chiefly in editorials that deal with domestic issues and the members themselves frequently write editorials on local issues, there is no correlation between circulation and the percentage of editorials devoted to Congress.

Connections between Nation and Locality

Some editorial writers connect nation and locality. Sometimes they do so by referring to national actions in an editorial about state or local developments; sometimes they do so by referring to local situations in an editorial about national or international affairs. In either case, the presence of such connections is an indication of an attempt to relate national developments to local concerns.

On that dimension, the *Lincoln Journal* was most likely to draw such connections, with 21.8 percent of its editorials linking state and nation. On the other end of the scale, the *Providence Journal* was least likely to do so, with only 8.6 percent of its editorials tying local concerns to national matters. Four of the papers fell into a narrow range in the middle, between 14.1 and 11.4 percent. Table 2.2 presents these results.

Those connections were almost exclusively drawn in editorials dealing with national matters. Only twenty-nine editorials linked international commentary with state or local concerns. Conversely, more than half the editorials dealing with Congress, the bureaucracy, or the Supreme Court involved such ties. But only a small proportion (139 out of 610) of editorials dealing with the president were connected to state

Table 2.2:   Number of Editorials Drawing Connections to State and Local Concerns in Selected Newspapers, 1994.

Newspaper	Total Editorials	Editorials Drawing Connections	Editorials Not Drawing Connections
Boise Idaho Statesman	778	142	636
Providence Journal	845	68	777
Lansing State Journal	689	78	611
Jackson Clarion-Ledger	973	136	837
Lincoln Journal	681	122	559
Fresno Bee	1,048	92	956
Raleigh News and Observer	906	110	796
Lexington Herald-Leader	550	68	482
Albuquerque Journal	678	95	583
Albany Times-Union	675	69	606

Source: Computed by author.

or local affairs. If we eliminate the international editorials (where the president is most likely to be featured), we still have a more than two-to-one imbalance (318 to 139). Connections are chiefly drawn in editorials dealing with national matters, and they are least likely to be drawn when the president is involved.

Circulation explains a great deal here. The larger papers are less likely to draw connections between national and international commentary and state and local matters. The correlation coefficient for that relationship is -.35. But that statistic is affected by the greater number of editorials published in the larger newspapers. The correlation between circulation and the percentage of editorials that draw such connections is -.76. The smaller the paper, the more likely the editors find it desirable to relate the developments under discussion to state and local interests.

The Top News and Editorial Topics

Editorials dealing with national and international issues were coded for the main topic addressed, and topics frequently addressed in these editorials were counted. Table 2.3 reports the number of editorials that dealt with these subjects. As one can readily see, they range from politics to policy to international affairs, with a surprising number of editorials on international matters—surprising, at least, to me.

Health care, welfare and welfare reform in its various guises, crime (chiefly the crime bill debated and passed during the summer of 1994), the federal budget deficit and related issues, and gun control received a great deal of editorial attention through the year. These five issues reflected the policy concerns editors in these papers had. Editors also commented extensively on political matters, such as Whitewater, the Clinton presidency, Congress and its operations, and the resurgence of the Republicans. International concerns such as Haiti, Bosnia, the Middle East peace process, North Korea, Russia, and international trade, comprised the rest of the most frequently discussed editorial topics. Tobacco-related matters also made the list, but that was chiefly the result of commentary in the Raleigh, North Carolina, and the Lexington, Kentucky, papers, where tobacco is as much a local issue as it is a national concern. Leaving those papers out, tobacco is not anywhere near the top of list.

This list does not resemble the Associated Press's list of the top ten news stories of 1994 very much at all.[13] Of the sixteen topics listed in

Table 2.3: Most Frequent Topics in Editorials in Selected Daily Newspapers, and the Wire Services' Top Ten Stories, 1994

Topic	Number of Editorials	On AP Top Ten List	On UPI Top Ten List
Health care	86	Yes	Yes
Haiti	80	Yes	Yes
Whitewater	75	No	No
Congress	68	No	No
Bosnia	62	No	Yes
Welfare	60	No	No
Crime	58	No	No
Federal budget	56	No	No
Clinton	51	No	No
Middle East	46	Yes	Yes
Gun control	44	No	No
North Korea	41	No	No
GOP resurgence	38	Yes	Yes
Russia	37	No	No
Tobacco	36	No	No
World trade	33	No	Yes
O. J. Simpson	28	Yes	Yes
Baseball strike	8	Yes	No
Susan Smith	6	Yes	No
Northridge earthquake	Not coded	Yes	No
Rwanda	23	Yes	Yes
South Africa	26	No	Yes
United Nations	Not coded	No	Yes
Northern Ireland	Not coded	No	Yes
Nancy Kerrigan	Not coded	Yes	No

Source: Computed by author.

table 2.3, only four appear on the AP top ten list. Its top story, the O. J. Simpson arrest and the subsequent judicial proceedings (the trial itself did not start until 1995), was discussed only twenty-eight times by the editors of these ten newspapers. Rwanda was the subject of twenty-three editorials, not in the top twenty of editorial topics. The list prepared by United Press International differed significantly from the AP list, but only five of its top news stories received a significant number of editorial comments. And the most frequently discussed issues among these editorials did not always appear on the wire services' lists. Whitewater, for instance, came up repeatedly in the editorials, as did welfare and the crime bill, but none of the three was significant enough to warrant inclusion on the wire services' list.

Some variation among newspapers in the running editorials on these most newsworthy topics clearly emerges. The *Lansing State Journal* included only three editorials that dealt with either the top politics subjects or the most frequently used international topics. It did, however, run twelve editorials referring to the leading policy matters. On the other hand, the *Lexington Herald-Leader*, similar in circulation to the Lansing paper, ran twenty editorials on the top political stories, while resembling the *State Journal* in its use of international and policy subjects in the editorials. A similar comparison can be made between two large papers, the *Fresno Bee* and the *Raleigh News Observer*. They published editorials at similar rates on policy and politics, but the Fresno daily presented its readers with seventy-two editorials about the rest of the world, while *News Observer* readers saw only ten such editorials in 1994. Generally, although circulation is positively associated with the number of editorials in each of these three categories, some wide variation exists, suggesting that considerations other than news values drives at least some of the editors' topic selection.

In no case does the list of the ten most frequently discussed topics in one paper's editorials over this year include more than four of the top stories on the AP list. No paper's most frequent editorial topics coincided with more than three of the leading stories on the UPI list. Whitewater, health-care reform, welfare, and Haiti were all among the ten most frequently discussed topics in seven of these newspapers. Bosnia, crime, North Korea, and gun control made the top ten list in five individual newspapers. Clearly, editors over this period were not more likely to comment more frequently on the top news stories as listed by the wire services.

In summary, this evidence supports seven conclusions. First, great variation in the number and percentage of editorials on national and international affairs appears among the papers included in this study. Second, this variation is largely accounted for by differences in circulation, with larger papers commenting more often, both proportionally and in number, on nonlocal issues. Third, the president and Congress are more likely to be discussed than the bureaucracy or the Supreme Court. Fourth, mention of the president is partially the result of the frequency with which he is referred to in editorials discussing international developments. Further, editors were more likely to draw connections to local and state concerns in editorials dealing with national than with international matters, and, sixth, those connections were even more likely to be drawn by newspapers with smaller circulations. Finally, the overlap between the top stories of the year as identified by the Associated Press and by United Press International, on the one hand, and the most frequently addressed editorial topics on the other, was not overly extensive. A number of issues received a great deal more editorial commentary than items appearing on the wire services' lists. If we look at the top topics for each newspaper separately, we find Whitewater, health-care reform, Haiti, and welfare among the top ten for seven of these newspapers.

DISCUSSION

Editors signal the significance of developments in part by their selection of topics for their daily editorials. But the expectation that "the attention paid to issues is quite consistent across various newspapers"[14] is not borne out by this examination of editorials published in 1994. Readers of some newspapers would rarely have had the opportunity to read editorials about international affairs or national politics. Readers of other newspapers would have, by contrast, been exposed to a sizable number of such commentaries. The signals readers of these different newspapers could have received are quite distinct—signals about the importance of these issues and signals of their relevance to the readers' concerns and interests.

That circulation explains most of the variation across these newspapers is not surprising. Larger papers have greater resources to devote to newsgathering, and they can therefore afford to cast their nets more widely. In doing so, they are more likely to consider subjects further afield from state and local concerns and wind up treating those topics in their editorial commentaries. Additionally, dailies with larger circulation serve a larger number of people with, perhaps, more diverse interests, so editorials on state and local matters would be appropriately supplemented with editorials on national and international developments. Finally, smaller papers with fewer resources may consciously choose to rely on syndicated columnists (or even reprinted editorials from other newspapers) for commentary on national and international affairs. Both the *Lexington Herald-Leader* and the *Albany Times-Union* seem to do so (but so does the substantially larger *Providence Journal*). The impact of circulation is therefore quite understandable.

I should repeat that the larger papers do not slight local and state matters in their editorials. The *Fresno Bee*, for instance, the paper with the most editorials on national and international news, still published almost six hundred editorials on state and local matters, which is more than five of the other papers in the study. The variation is more a result of increasing attention to the nation and the world, not the result of reducing commentary on state and locality in order to address national and international issues. It is for this reason, too, that circulation accounts for so much of the variance in addressing nonlocal matters; larger papers are more likely to be able to devote additional resources to those concerns.

Several pieces of evidence apply directly to the main concern raised earlier: the extent to which selection of editorial topics is news-driven or audience-driven. First, when editors draw connections between the events they are commenting on and state and local considerations, concern with the readership is evident. The development under discussion in the editorial, in other words, is not, per se, relevant to the newspaper's readers; instead, the editor finds it appropriate to make the linkage explicit. Frequently, too, although I did not code explicitly for this point, national activities involving local residents (e.g., members of the House of Representatives, members of the cabinet, etc.) are more likely to become subjects for editorials than the newsworthiness of these developments themselves warrant. The signal the editors send in these cases is that the national and international developments are significant for the readers to attend to because they relate directly to local issues or personalities.

Second, some national and international events were more likely to be subjects of editorials than others, but the most frequently discussed issues were not necessarily on the wire services' top stories list. They do, however, seem to be significant stories, nationally and internationally.

They may have been very graphic, such as the Northridge earthquake, with its impact, its human interest angle, and its timeliness. But they were frequently ongoing developments where the cumulative news value was just as great. Editorial writers, for instance, frequently discussed the long debate in Washington over the 1994 crime bill, commenting on the disagreements between President Clinton and legislators in Congress and on the merit of various elements of the proposal. The absence of many of the wire services' top stories from the list of the most frequently discussed editorial topics is not, then, automatic evidence that editors are not partially news-driven in their topic selection. Their commentaries on Whitewater in its early stages and on welfare reform and gun control reflect, I think, more a news-driven choice than an audience-driven one.

Third, the extent to which the same topics appear on the "most frequently discussed" list of editorial topics for the newspapers taken separately indicates that in deciding to comment on these issues, the editors were not responding to local concerns alone. Whitewater and Haiti affected few if any localities directly, yet most newspapers commented frequently on these issues. Editors throughout the nation seemed to have responded similarly to the value of devoting an editorial to these subjects. Local concerns cannot explain it; this selection of topics reflects their news value.

Several implications emerge. For one thing, despite the need and desire of local newspapers to serve distinct local audiences, a need we see demonstrated by the extent to which editorial topic selection is audience-driven, a significant set of editorial topics was selected because of national news value. Some consistency of topics comes out across the nation. If Cohen is right, that the media "is stunningly successful in telling us what to think about,"[15] editors across the nation are asking their readers to think about the same issues.

For another, it is evident that editors take their responsibility seriously. Gun control, Bosnia, welfare reform, and the federal budget present much more significant and longer-lasting concerns than many of the other issues on the Associated Press's list of the year's top stories. The Nancy Kerrigan ice skating incident, the Susan Smith murder case, and the baseball strike, not to mention the O. J. Simpson *contretemps*, present evanescent issues, heavy on human interest but low in policy implications. While editors may have devoted extensive coverage to these developments in their news columns, they used their editorial columns on more momentous issues. To careful readers, the signal must be hard to miss: it's nice to know about Tonya Harding's escapades, but welfare reform is more important to think about.

The potential effect on public discourse of this pattern of topic selection in editorials is noteworthy. Despite the melodramatic nature of his argument in *Amusing Ourselves to Death*, I still like the definition of public discourse Neil Postman offers there: "our political, religious, informational and commercial forms of conversation."[16] Because state and local policymakers and political activists are likely to be especially attentive readers of editorials, editors' selections of topics facilitate the entry of these issues into the public discourse in localities across the nation. That discourse is more national than it might be because of the similarities from newspaper to newspaper in cities across the nation.

To be sure, there are regional variations. The emphasis on tobacco issues in the Kentucky and North Carolina papers has already been noted. The Fresno and Albuquerque papers were more likely to comment on immigration issues. And these two papers, along with the *Boise Idaho Statesman*, ran more editorials on land use and grazing fees on federal lands, long-standing western concerns. But these regional issues, reflecting local differences, stand alongside national concerns. That diversity is to be expected. But even despite the frequency with which some papers addressed these issues, they still provided their readers with numerous editorials on national issues.

The differences between larger and smaller newspapers, however, suggest strongly that people living in cities served by lower circulation newspapers should supplement their media consumption with other sources.[17] To a great extent, editors in smaller newspapers do not alert their readers to the significance of the national and international issues of the day by their selection of topics for their editorials. If those signals are not sent, and not received, readers of such newspapers are less well prepared to participate in our national political conversation about those issues.

NOTES

1. "Now, the Real Test in Haiti," *Albany (New York) Times-Union*, 20 September 1994, A(10).

2. "Triumph in Haiti," *Raleigh (North Carolina) News and Observer*, 20 September 1994.

3. "Air Safety Can't Wait," *Raleigh (North Carolina) News and Observer*, 16 December 1994.

4. "Time to Reregulate?" *Providence (Rhode Island) Journal*, 16 December 1994, A(16).

5. For discussions of objectivity, see Daniel C. Hallin, *The "Uncensored War": The Media and Vietnam* (New York: Oxford University Press, 1986), 63–75; Bernard Roshco, *Newsmaking* (Chicago: University of Chicago Press, 1975); Michael Schudson, *Discovering the News: A Social History of American Newspapers* (New York: Basic Books, 1978) esp. 3–10; and Dan Schiller, *Objectivity and the News: The Public and the Rise of Commercial Journalism* (Philadelphia: University of Pennsylvania Press, 1981).

6. Doris Graber, *Mass Media and American Politics*, 5th ed., (Washington, D.C.: Congressional Quartlery, 1997), 106–8; Jan Pons Vermeer, *"For Immediate Release": Candidate Press Releases in American Political Campaigns* (Westport, Conn.: Greenwood Press, 1982), 16–19.

7. W. Lance Bennett, "An Introduction to Journalism Norms and Representation of Politics," *Political Communication* 13, no. 4 (October/December 1996): 373.

8. W. Lance Bennett, "Toward a Theory of Press-State Relations in the United States," *Journal of Communication* 40, no. 2 (spring 1990): 106.

9. See Bennett, "Toward a Theory of Press-State Relations," and the symposium on "Journalism Norms and News Construction" he and Timothy Cook co-edited in *Political Communication* 13, no. 4 (October/December 1996): 373–481.

10. Walter Lippmann, *Public Opinion* (New York: Harcourt Brace, 1922), 364.

11. Graber, *Mass Media*, 5.

12. Jan P. Vermeer, "Themes in Local Newspaper Editorials: Newsworthiness and Editorial Commentary" (paper presented at the annual meeting of the Southwest Political Science Association, Dallas, Tex., March 1995).

13. "Wire Services Pick Top Stories of 1994," *Editor and Publisher*, 7 January 1995, 54.

14. Jon A. Krosnick and Laura A. Brannon, "New Evidence on News Media Priming: In 1992, It Was the Economy!" (paper presented at the annual meeting of the American Political Science Association, Chicago, Ill., 1995), 3.

15. Bernard C. Cohen, *The Press and Foreign Policy* (Princeton, N.J.: Princeton University Press, 1963), 13.

16. Neil Postman, *Amusing Ourselves to Death: Public Discourse in the Age of Show Business* (New York: Viking, 1985), 28.

17. For general differences between residents of smaller and larger cities, see J. Eric Oliver, "City Size and Civic Involvement in Metropolitan America," *American Political Science Review* 94 (June 2000): 361–73.

Chapter Three

Congress:
Is It National or Is It Local?

Congress is not widely liked. Even when it pursues laudable goals, the press and the public remain skeptical about the institution. "Trying to safeguard blessings that Nature effortlessly provided," the *Raleigh News & Observer* noted, "Congress . . . produced some of the most tangled, tortured, obscure regulations ever written, and some of the costliest to implement."[1] Congress is a victim of its members, who can potentially embark "on a one-man sabotage operation"[2] when they deem it necessary, at a cost to rational national policy making. They are, in the view of some in the local press, misguided; editors regard them dubiously: many have "hung around too long, building a tidy little empire . . . ," becoming part of an "imperial Congress."[3]

The litany of complaints with Congress goes on. Editors at the *Jackson Clarion-Ledger* told their readers that balancing the federal budget is a matter of "will." The problem is that "lawmakers have consistently shown a lack of willpower when it comes to spending the taxpayers' money."[4] The *Albuquerque Journal* complained of Congress playing politics with the crime bill being debated over the summer of 1994: "congressional politics has degenerated from art to a dismal science where money is what makes things possible, including bad legislation."[5] Editors at the *Boise Idaho Statesman* despaired of the "partisan bickering over health care" that same summer. "This display of chaos, desperation and blatant self-interest is what fuels the public's 'throw the bums out' mentality on Election Day,"[6] they told their readers.

The commentary was not all negative, of course. When Senate Majority Leader George Mitchell (D-Maine) announced his retirement effective at the end of the year, the *Fresno Bee* lauded his "concern, hard work, and honesty that earned him the respect of both sides of the aisle."[7] The *Lexington Herald-Leader* credited a federal mandate, a device generally maligned by state and local officials, for the Kentucky legislature's reversing its decision not to make seatbelt use mandatory. "Would the bill have been passed without the threat of lost federal funds? Maybe. Maybe not. But obviously, this federal mandate didn't hurt."[8] Albuquerque editors acknowledged the contribution of the Brady Law—requiring background checks for those seeking to purchase handguns—in keeping a gun out of the hand of one particular felon. "Put a notch on the gun for the Brady Law—another notch, actually," they said. "The law without question is keeping many people with criminal or mental records or pending felony charges from buying guns at regulated shops," a result the paper said was worth the five-day delay in purchasing guns, a delay it termed "no great inconvenience."[9]

In this predominantly negative picture, partially countered with some positive strokes with which local newspaper editors paint Congress, the editors resemble the rest of the nation. The public clearly thinks the worst of Congress, even though people will grudgingly admit that Congress has occasionally done the right thing. To some extent, editors both lead and reflect public opinion about Congress. In this chapter, I will examine the treatment Congress is accorded in the daily press. It will become clear that uniformly across the nation Congress is depicted in unflattering ways; the most representative of institutions in the national government is seen as remote, unresponsive, and, indeed, unrepresentative, local members excepted. And yet a possibility of redemption persists. The institution can be saved.

In other words, editors of these local daily newspapers do not see Congress as an institution that effectively and routinely responds to the needs of the public as the editors see them. Even more, editors see Congress responding to unimportant needs, or see worthwhile policy objectives sidetracked or derailed for political or regional purposes for the benefit of special interests or narrow segments of the population, at the expense of everyday hard-working folks such as those who read the editors' newspapers. Were it not for the efforts of the hometown members, the situation would be even worse. Just ask these editors.

PERCEPTIONS OF CONGRESS

Congress occupies a unique and ambiguous place in the national political system. It is at once the national legislature, with responsibilities for determining policies that will guide the country as a whole, whether economic, social, military, or fiscal, and also a gathering of representatives from various states and localities who bargain with each other to gain advantages, avoid costs, and influence national policies in ways that will benefit (or at least not harm) the folks back home. The dual function sets Congress apart from both the presidency and the Supreme Court, both of which have primary responsibilities toward national policy, and little if any concern with a geographically defined constituency.

Perhaps the bureaucracy comes closest to facing a comparable dilemma, in that some agencies, such as the Federal Aviation Administration, must both regulate and foster the industries they monitor. But only members of Congress are so dependent on political support in their circumscribed constituencies. Representatives and Senators owe their positions not to their success in policy making for the nation as a whole, nor to their willingness to cooperate with their colleagues and their political parties. Neither do they owe their seats to presidential influence or patronage from the White House. They come to Congress and return to Congress because they win their local elections. To be sure, national partisan trends affect both the likelihood that contributors will provide the large sums of money needed to wage a reelection campaign and the chance that a well-qualified, well-known challenger may emerge as an opponent in November.[10] But members' political survival depends on their own efforts in building and maintaining political support in the district or state.

Legislators spend significant resources to do so. They dedicate a large portion of their staff's time and attention to constituents' requests for assistance. In fact, some members go out of their way to solicit such requests.[11] They figure they can only gain thereby. Their office can usually help the constituent, the representatives get good word-of-mouth recommendations, and constituents perceive them in a nonpolitical, nonpartisan role, as a true servant of the people. Legislators also devote resources to bringing pork barrel projects to the state or district, and the concrete (no pun intended) results help them point with pride to the benefits they brought home. Furthermore, making frequent trips home, meeting with constituents when they visit Washington, and answering calls and letters from the district place additional demands on a legislator's time.

On the other hand, making national policy constitutes, unavoidably, a no-win situation for most legislators. Working diligently for the good of the nation yields few rewards back home, unless there are distinct and clear benefits to the district or state itself. Rarely are one member's contributions to major legislation distinct enough or pivotal enough for much credit-claiming. Rarely are constituents, even attentive ones, aware of the legislator's work behind the scenes, and even final votes on passage may not be common knowledge. Further, legislators become vulnerable to criticism from electoral opponents for putting the nation ahead of the district if they spend too much time on national policy.

On balance, the rewards of national policy making pale in comparison to those coming from cultivating the constituency. As a result, most legislators would rather be perceived as serving their district and winning reelection than seen as ignoring local needs in favor of national concerns and risk losing their seats. They value the work of the institution less than the efforts needed to serve the district and win reelection.

Most people have only a vague and limited understanding of Congress and few measures by which to judge its performance. They know enough, however, to know they do not like it.[12] Nevertheless, despite the low regard in which people hold the institution, incumbents generally enjoy marked popularity and win reelection at very high rates, even in "anti-incumbent" election years such as 1992 and 1994. People love their representatives; they dislike the body.[13] This ambivalence is reflected in the widespread support for term limits across the nation, even in the face of the continuing reelection of most incumbents. A plausible interpretation is that voters like their own incumbents but wish people in other districts would stop reelecting their representatives, who implicitly get the blame for all the problems voters perceive in Congress.

The distinction between the public's evaluation of the legislator and of the legislature is not new. The academic literature on the electorate's favorable assessments of congressional incumbents needs no review here;[14] suffice it to note that the public's preference for incumbents has been well documented. The dissatisfaction with Congress as a whole, however, has not been so thoroughly studied. Many think the public's disillusionment with Congress is of rather recent origin, another product of a post–Watergate mentality. Mark Rozell, however, has demonstrated that the press has rarely viewed Congress as a very positive institution during the twentieth century.[15] Hibbing and Theiss-Morse's study points out why: the more open the process, the less the public likes what it sees.[16]

Editors share this ambivalence, and in their editorials in 1994 they communicated these outlooks to their readers. It becomes clear, upon reading these editorials, that editors generally comment favorably on their local members of Congress but less favorably on other members, that they criticize congressional procedures, often using extraordinary situations as if they were typical of Congress, and that they evaluate Congress chiefly on the results it produces. In general, editors of local daily newspapers see Congress as an integral part of the Washington establishment, an institution whose members simply do not understand real life back home.

Members of Congress

Members of Congress from a newspaper's own circulation area generally receive favorable editorial commentary. Their press releases announcing federal grants to community projects generate additional mentions, and their votes and other actions on bills potentially affecting the locality rate plaudits and recognition. One might, however, expect just the opposite. Since the local members are precisely the legislators who are most likely to read the editorials most closely, editorial writers have a great opportunity to chastise the area's representatives and to point out their mistaken judgments. Criticizing another state's senators, for instance, would likely have little effect. Hometown legislators would have more reason to take the paper's corrections seriously, because their own constituents could be among the readers. Nevertheless, editorials in local daily newspapers attract favorable editorial commentary, with only rare exceptions.

Those positive assessments crop up chiefly in two contexts for the period examined here. One set emerges, unsurprisingly, during "endorsement season," when the newspapers anoint a contender in the November elections for any seat being contested. These editorials portray local House members and home state Senators as hard-working and principled servants of the people. The second set crops up during discussions of congressional activity (or inactivity, as the case may be) on issues of vital concern to the locality—vital at least in the eyes of the editorial writers. The final passage of a bill containing a provision keeping a nearby military base open or protecting a local industry from undue and oppressive regulation resulted from the diligent work of

Representative X or Senator Y. Some examples will make the pattern obvious.

The *Jackson Clarion-Ledger* endorsed Trent Lott's reelection to the U.S. Senate, despite their opposition to him six years earlier. But in 1994 it pointed to his "commitment, dedication and effectiveness" in Congress, noting that he "studies, works hard and he listens." Perhaps most importantly, he has "the fortitude to balance the state's interests with national goals."[17] Similarly, Michael McNulty (D-N.Y.) received the *Albany Times-Union* endorsement for reelection, because he "has risen in stature and responsibility in the House" without losing touch with his district. In fact, McNulty "always seems to be in [his constituents'] midst, lending an attentive ear to their concerns."[18] Long-time GOP representative Doug Bereuter won the *Lincoln Journal*'s endorsement for reelection, not because "Bereuter and the *Journal* always agree," but because the paper respects "an incumbent who can make up his own mind and go his own way."[19]

There are, however, exceptions to the kind words of editorial writers about members running for reelection. Perhaps the most scathing nonendorsement was the *Boise Idaho Statesman*'s frank disavowal of Larry LaRocco. Despite endorsing him in previous elections, the paper took issue with Mr. LaRocco's response to allegations of sexual discrimination. Mr. LaRocco did not admit to misconduct, and the paper expected him to acknowledge the error of his ways. As a result, "the newspaper cannot bring itself to now support a candidate who has proved himself unworthy of the public trust." Despite "important public policy differences" the paper has with LaRocco's opponent, and despite his "good record," the paper decided that "LaRocco has . . . shown voters that he cannot be trusted to tell the truth."[20] Character trumps policy.

Kind comments on legislators from the local area also frequently emerge from editorial commentary on bills that successfully make it to final passage. In these instances, editorial writers find that it was the efforts by the hometown representative or the state's own Senator that made the difference between passage and defeat or between inclusion of helpful provisions or their exclusion. One cannot, it would seem from reading between the lines of these editorials, expect legislators from the rest of the country to understand the importance of these provisions and these bills. The assumption that such legislation benefits the nation as a whole as well as the local area is often, but not always, left unstated.

For instance, when the House of Representatives finally included some funds in a crime bill to compensate states for their costs in jailing suspected illegal immigrants, the *Fresno Bee* gave credit to Representative Tony Beilenson, while recognizing that the Senate still had to act. Beilenson, the *Bee* pointed out, "was engaged in this battle [for federal funds] long before it became politically fashionable."[21] Sometimes just working hard for a bill the newspaper favors generates positive publicity in the editorial columns. Senator Dirk Kempthorne (R-Idaho), the *Boise Idaho Statesman* pointed out, was "close to accomplishing a major reform" when his bill to eliminate unfunded mandates attracted over fifty cosponsors.[22] The paper emphasized Kempthorne's junior status in noting that passage of the bill would be a feather in the cap of even a long-time Senator.

Sometimes legislators get credit—and positive comments—for blocking a governmental agency from making a wrong move, at least wrong from the paper's perspective. Both of New Mexico's senators, Pete Dominici (R) and Jeff Bingaman (D), and Representative Joe Skeen (R-N.M.), received kind words for their efforts to put language in the bill for the 1995 appropriations for the Department of the Interior that would keep the lunchroom at the Carlsbad Caverns open. The *Lincoln Journal* likewise gave Senator Jim Exon (D-Nebr.) plaudits for exposing the General Services Administration's plan to spend almost a half million dollars to make a Lincoln federal office building earthquake proof, in an area that "has not felt tremors that did much more than jiggle the crockery since 1877."[23]

Lest these examples seem overly one-sided, I must point out the severity with which the *Raleigh News & Observer* treated Senator Jesse Helms (R-N.C.) during the year. When Helms claimed that an amendment he introduced to the 1994 crime bill would "solve North Carolina's prison woes," the paper called it "baloney" and described Helms's maneuver as "playing political games."[24] When Helms blocked the nomination of Robert Pastor as ambassador to Panama, the *News & Observer* accused him of trying to "disrupt the smooth running of his country's foreign affairs," only because Helms "has never gotten over the Panama Canal Treaty." No one's interests are being served by Helms's tactics, the paper argued, "except one senator['s] from North Carolina."[25] Most newspapers, however, save such critical comments for legislators from other states and localities.

The editorials make relatively infrequent negative assessments of other legislators, chiefly because proximity and familiarity are important news values even in selecting topics for editorials. But when a senator as familiar as Helms speaks thoughtlessly, newspapers across the country are quick to use their editorials to express their outrage. When the senator was quoted to the effect that President Clinton was unfit to serve as Commander in Chief and, later, that Clinton would be well advised to have a bodyguard while visiting a military base in North Carolina, paper after paper responded. The *Albuquerque Journal* called the remarks "[a]t best, . . . insulting[;] [a]t worst, Helms' remarks could promote sedition."[26] The *Lexington Herald-Leader* called him "a loose senatorial cannon."[27] A later Lexington editorial summed it up: "No matter what, you can be thankful that Helms isn't *your* Senator."[28]

Occasionally, other negative depiction surfaces. When Representative Alcee Hastings (D-Fla.) suggests a controversial solution to the Haitian crisis (make Haiti a U.S. commonwealth like Puerto Rico), the *Providence Journal* identified him right at the start as the "onetime federal judge who was tried and acquitted of bribery charges."[29] The debate over agreeing to the GATT accords also generated some less than flattering portrayals. Senator Robert Dole (R-Kans.) was applauded when he "blessedly . . . decided to stop playing political games,"[30] while Senator Fritz Hollings (D-S.C.) was accused of a "one-man sabotage operation . . . for the narrowest reason: To shield his state's textile industry from foreign competition."[31] When distant legislators get notices on the editorial page, they rarely get favorable reviews.

Congressional Procedures

To most citizens, the task of legislators appears clear and straightforward: recognize the nation's problems and adopt workable solutions to them, so that the national interest can be served. Scholars of the legislative process, however, consider lawmaking "a complicated and often harrowing process"[32] not easily yielding clear and effective legislative solutions to the vexing problems of the day. By 1994, "[c]omplaints about structures and procedures were legion"[33] among the public and some political activists as well. Dissatisfaction with Congress seemed ultimately to be focused on the way the institution itself operated.

Editorial writers seem to share the public's perception. To them, if Congress does not act or does not pass appropriate bills, there is clearly both a problem and a cause for that problem. Archaic procedures, partisan bickering, pandering to special interests, and pork barrel legislation comprise the core of editorial objections to Congress and its procedures.

Editors would like to see more meaningful floor debate take place in Congress. When, as an experiment, the House of Representatives offered a floor debate on health-care reform following the "Oxford model," the *Albany Times-Union* responded enthusiastically. "Perhaps never before," it said, "have so many millions of Americans been treated to such a prolonged, and lively, examination" of a legislative proposal.[34] And although the *Raleigh News & Observer* was less complimentary ("more a forensic food fight than the polite, erudite formal exchange optimists had hoped for"), it nevertheless conceded that it was "certainly more revealing and more informative than watching arcane wrangles over obscure amendments."[35] The more usual procedure in Congress evinces the "partisan bickering[,] . . . chaos, desperation, and blatant self-interest" about which the public frequently complains.[36]

Any changes in congressional procedures, however, should make sense, according to these editorial writers. No "supermajority" vote to raise taxes should be instituted, the *Fresno Bee* said, because it is "antidemocratic on its face and sets a troubling precedent," not to mention that it "diminishes the accountability" of legislators to the public.[37] Improvements that make sense would increase the likelihood that Congress will act effectively with the nation's problems.

In that light, the *Albuquerque Journal* argued for an end to "commemorative" legislation, such as naming a "National Scleroderma Awareness Month." The paper called it "absurd" for Congress to devote time to such matters when it "always seems so short of time to complete specific acts of governance."[38] The Lincoln, Nebraska, paper suggested that following its state's move to biennial budgeting would be a good step for Congress, a change proposed by the Joint Committee on the Organization of Congress. It was reform at the state level "that made government more efficient," and "[t]here's every reason to think that biennial budgets at the federal level would offer similar efficiencies."[39]

Editorial opposition to pork barrel legislation is so expected that only one quotation might serve to buttress the inference that editors think of such provisions as symptomatic of all that's wrong with Congress today. The *Albuquerque Journal* contrasted the plight of average citizens "who have to scrimp and save to make ends meet" with "the propensity of some" members of Congress to "fund pet projects" of "questionable merit" simply because they "benefit their home states."[40] And of course it goes without saying that it is members from other states who do so too frequently.

Special interests (rarely just "interest groups") receive particular con-
demnation, in large part because it is so easy to contrast the benefits to
an identifiable group with a more amorphous national interest. In 1994,
a proposal to reform campaign finance provided editorial writers with
an opportunity to vent their frustration at the undue (in their eyes) influence of groups who fund congressional campaigns for reelection.
Without such reform, "legislation . . . becomes a commodity to be
bartered, twisted and shaped to suit those who have spread around the
most dollars," the Raleigh paper said.[41] The same paper argued later
that campaign contributors "leav[e] the understandable impression with
voters that their representatives . . . offer special interest groups the
hope that generosity will be rewarded with access to power."[42] A dis-
closure bill, requiring lobbyists to report whom they represent and what
issues they are working on, ran into a roadblock in the Senate; as a result, "an army of highly-paid lobbyists [can] descend on the nation's
representatives [to] wine, dine and otherwise seduce them," to the detri-
ment of the public interest.[43] Who, then, looks out for the good of all?
these editorial writers implicitly ask.

Some editors expressed hope that the 1994 elections would lead to
some positive changes. The *Lansing State Journal* saw the vote as the
"proper judgment on Congress as an institution badly in need of a shak-
ing."[44] "The voters," the *Fresno Bee* noted, "have given a congressional
party accustomed to opposition the responsibility of delivering real an-
swers to the country's problems, not two years of partisan sniping."[45]
Change was the theme: "Whatever else the American people meant
with their votes Tuesday," the *Albany Times Union* said, "they have
clearly had it with the posturing and bickering of the past two years."[46]
The intervening years have not shown that editors' optimism has been
rewarded.

Legislative Results

Citizens, it seems, want Congress to produce solid, acceptable solutions
to the nation's problems, regardless of the difficulties congressional
procedures pose. "Congress as a whole," Davidson and Oleszek point
out, "is judged by policies and results."[47] When Congress does not act
to deal with issues that cry out for resolution, because, say, there is no
consensus on an appropriate response, members have no legislation to
point to as an accomplishment. Failure to agree on a bill that the president, governors, and other leaders acknowledge as a sound response to

a problem indicates that, once again, Congress has proven itself inadequate at a time of urgency, thereby reinforcing negative stereotypes of Congress. Congress's public image, then, depends in part on its ability to legislate.

The year 1994 presented Congress with two major opportunities to act. One came in the form of a presidential initiative: President Clinton's proposal to reform the nation's health-care funding system. The second was the crime bill, a large, complex set of policies that would address the public's concern with violent crime. How Congress dealt with these issues differed; one was ultimately never passed, while the second won approval and a subsequent presidential signature. The former was chiefly a Democratic proposal; the latter reflected Republican priorities more closely. Editorial commentary on these bills along the way will tell us more about the way Congress is depicted in daily newspapers.

These concerns became frequent editorial fodder for editors to turn and return to. The insights into the inner workings of the legislative branch provided examples that editors could point to with disdain or with pride. More importantly, editors could compare the needs that the proposals emphasized, in both health care and in crime, with the ungainly and awkward strides Congress made toward dealing with those needs. These issues gave editors an opportunity to criticize congressional procedures and, ultimately, congressional action.

President Clinton's proposal to reform health care in the nation came before Congress during the 1993 session, but extended examination of the proposal that emerged from the administration did not occur until 1994. Three kinds of issues came forward during this period: Did health care need to be reformed? Were the proposed reforms appropriate solutions to the problem? Did the drawbacks of the proposal outweigh its anticipated advantages? The administration's position was crystal clear. Health care was in drastic need of reform, both because of its costs and because of the large numbers of people without health insurance. Some type of managed care with universal coverage, funded by the national government, was likely the most effective way to deal with the problem, although Clinton left open the possibility of accepting other workable solutions. Whatever the disadvantages, the administration saw the problem as severe enough to more than counter the disadvantages that might result.

Republicans disagreed vehemently. They disputed each of these points. The health-care system, despite its faults, was working acceptably well. Other more limited solutions to cure the ailments from which the system suffered, within the context of private enterprise, seemed more attractive. Finally, the proposed reforms added another layer of bureaucracy and the costs could skyrocket, threatening whatever chances there were for ultimately balancing the federal budget and bringing taxes down. Or so Republicans said.

The issue became a dominant one over the summer of 1994. Interest groups, especially health-care groups such as pharmaceutical associations and health insurance companies, lobbied Congress extensively. More significantly, these groups also conducted a massive advertising campaign to emphasize the negative elements they saw in the administration's proposal. Television commercials starring "Harry and Louise," portraying an average American middle-aged couple, depicted the proposed reforms as both overly complicated, and therefore typical of government programs, and unclear in their possible implications, thereby raising fears of the unknown. Because the issue became so prominent, citizens could hardly escape hearing about it.

With the issue so high on the public's agenda, so prominently a part of the president's program, and so vigorously contested by Republicans in Congress, editorial writers pounced on the topic frequently over the course of the year.

When Congress began to examine Clinton's health-care proposal in March of 1994, editors were generally optimistic, not necessarily about the chances of a major legislative accomplishment, but about members seriously tackling the issue. When a House subcommittee acted on a proposed amendment to the plan, the *Jackson Clarion-Ledger* editors, for example, called the matter one "of monumental importance," even though it was "overshadowed by the hype over an Arkansas S&L that failed years ago."[48] Although they doubted that Clinton's plan was the way to go, calling it "a federal takeover of 14 percent of the economy," *Boise Idaho Statesman* editors recognized that "better health care" was indeed "possible."[49] And in Providence, Rhode Island, editorial readers were assured that "[s]urely [Congress] can come up with something relatively simple" to provide health-care coverage for everyone.[50] But optimistic forecasts do not always come true.

By late June, the *Lincoln Journal* voiced its concern that health-care reform would fall victim to congressional gridlock. The editorial writers were specifically chagrined to find that legislators have "mirror[ed] a public mood that has drifted between uneasy support and uneasy opposition," opposition that resulted from a campaign of "disinformation" waged "by people who don't want, and never did want, any changes in the health care system at all."[51] It echoed the *Fresno Bee*'s earlier observation that "the most important question . . . is no longer what kind of reform will emerge from Congress, but whether any will," adding that "failure to reach agreement now would be a tragedy."[52]

It was clear to most observers by August that health-care reform would not be passed. No consensus had emerged, "as sure a sign as any that Congress has little chance of enacting reform this year," according to the *Lansing State Journal*.[53] Reform had fallen victim to partisan politics, at least in the eyes of the editorialists at the *Albany Times Union*. They blamed Senate Minority Leader Robert Dole and Senator Phil Gramm for trying to build support among the Republican right wing for their "presumed candida[cies] for their party's presidential nomination" by blocking real legislative work on the health-care reform version drawn up by Majority Leader George Mitchell of Maine. "All this may be good partisan politics," the editors noted, "but it's lousy public service."[54] The *Jackson Clarion-Ledger* editors, in their epitaph for health-care reform, called on voters to "say who gets the blame/credit." It was, so they said, "finger-pointing time in Washington."[55]

The omnibus crime bill of 1994 was also subject to intense partisan conflict in Congress. Crime had become a major issue throughout the nation, and national politicians felt it important to take a strong anti-crime stance, despite the local nature of most criminal activity. Republicans especially had hit crime hard as an issue over the previous years (the infamous "Willie Horton" spot during the 1988 presidential campaign being the most vivid example). But in 1994 President Clinton stole the anticrime limelight by urging Congress to adopt a far-reaching and complex bill that provided money to states and localities for additional police officers and prisons, funded crime prevention programs, including "midnight basketball" leagues, and made more federal crimes subject to the death penalty.

The road to passage was both bumpy and tortuous. Gun control posed one hurdle. The Senate incorporated an anti-assault weapon provision into its version of the crime bill when it approved an amendment offered by Senator Dianne Feinstein (D-Calif.), but the House considered it separately. To the surprise of many observers, among them the editors of the *Fresno Bee*,[56] the House passed the ban by two votes, despite heavy lobbying by the National Rifle Association. In August, opponents to the bill in the House managed, by a procedural maneuver, to prevent the House from voting on the conference report. But the idea of passing a crime bill in an election year proved too attractive, and ultimately the legislation wound up on Clinton's desk for his signature.

Unlike the health-care reform bill, where citizens and politicians disagreed about whether a problem even existed, consensus on the crime problem prevailed. "Americans are fed up with rampant crime," the *Jackson Clarion-Ledger* noted. "They want action."[57] Albuquerque editors called crime "an issue of great concern to Americans,"[58] and in Fresno, editorial readers were told that the nation was "understandably worried about crime."[59] Even the editors of the *Lansing State Journal*, who so rarely commented on national political affairs, noted that "Americans do want some sort of anti-crime action out of Congress," and they hoped that it would include an assault weapons ban.[60]

But editors were equally disturbed by many of the bill's provisions, elements that they thought would do little if anything to affect the nation's crime rate. The editors of the *Albany Times-Union* called the increase in the number of federal crimes punishable by death "mostly symbolic, and otherwise empty,"[61] because violent crime tends to fall under state jurisdiction. The *Bee* editors worried about "the bill's intrusive mandates" on states' decisions about sentencing, for example.[62] The *Lincoln Journal* warned readers that the bill's "three strikes" provision "sounds fierce, but it may stick taxpayers with the bill for warehousing geriatric prisoners who are long past the phase of their lives when they pose a threat to society."[63]

Editors were more perturbed by the depiction of the legislative process that congressional work on the crime bill manifested. It has, said the *Raleigh News & Observer*, "given Americans a good picture of self-serving politics at work."[64] How was the bill "self-serving?" It was a "Christmas tree with a badge,"[65] "a Christmas tree of [federal] programs" intruding into state prerogatives,[66] a "spectacularly expensive . . . Christmas tree that people are hanging things on,"[67] and, to shift metaphors, a bill with a great deal of "'pork' or excessive spending in it."[68] As a result, the bill became a vehicle to pass out benefits, so that it wound up "having something for everyone."[69] Notably missing are concerns with crime itself and with doing what is best for all. Much of the spending authorized by the bill "was directed not at crime at all, but at dubious social programs," complained the editors of the *Albany Times Union* later.[70] The *Lexington Herald-Leader* concluded that "[t]his bill is more about politics in an election year than it is about crime."[71]

It comes somewhat as a surprise, then, to discover that the editors
were pleased by the outcome. The "result is a pretty good crime bill";[72]
"[f]or all the posturing and so-called pork, the crime bill achieves some
progress,"[73] said the *Fresno Bee* editors. Their colleagues in Providence
agreed, despite the "fatuousness" included in the bill.[74] More significant than the content to the *Bee* editors, however, was the simple fact
that the bill passed. It signaled "the federal government's ability to address an issue of major public concern"[75] and demonstrated "that major
problems can be addressed."[76] Had the bill not passed, the public would
have seen it "as further evidence that when it comes to the really vexing problems that plague the nation, government is helpless and con-
fused."[77] "Most . . . of the bill represents sound public policy."[78]

CONCLUSION

Despite the range of newspapers represented here, the editorials painted
a relatively coherent portrait of Congress in action. Stubbornly negative
in its terms, editors see Congress as a captive, both of its procedures and
of the interests that would hamstring it in its duty to legislate for the
public good. Whether those interests reflected the influence of lobbyists
or of well-entrenched members themselves, they clearly—clearly, at
least, to the editors—worked to undermine the efforts of those few who
would seek to pursue the national interest. When Congress does indeed
accomplish something, it is likely to be greeted by surprise and aston-
ishment.

That portrait of Congress is one we have come to expect, given the
nature of commentary and reporting on Congress in the national media.
Mark Rozell characterizes it as "a debilitating cynicism that potentially
undermines the foundation of representative government."[79] Waves of
scandal reporting wash across the nation—the House Bank scandal, the
bribe-taking of some members during "Abscam," the Keating Five de-
bacle—the list goes on and on. But one will not find waves of praise for
congressional action in the national media. It is seemingly one-sided
and negative. Davidson and Oleszek put the point harshly: "Journalistic hit-and-run specialists, especially newsmagazines, editorial writers,
and talk show hosts, perpetuate a cartoonish stereotype: an irresponsi-
ble and somewhat sleazy body of people approximating Woodrow Wilson's caustic description of the House as 'a disintegrated mass of jar-
ring elements.'"[80]

   The survey of the content of local daily newspaper editorials conducted here, however, forces us to moderate that impression. The
conclusion that extensive negative commentary of Congress leads to
a negative appraisal of that institution may not follow. If the perspectives in daily newspaper editorials about Congress are any guide,
readers can find a great deal of negative commentary on Congress as
a whole, tempered by emphasis on the positive contributions made
by their own representatives. The coverage in the national media,
where no media outlet has much incentive to consistently praise "local" representatives, is much more uniformly critical and negative.
Yes, Congress has problems, but these difficulties can be surmounted
through the efforts of strong, effective public servants such as the
members from the paper's own area.

   Further, these editors implicitly put forward the notion that the problems Congress experiences result from two forces working in tandem.
First, Congress's negative attributes follow from the narrow parochialism and local favoritism *other* members display. Gridlock is the product of *other* members refusing to compromise. Bills laden with pork for
specific districts are needed because *other* members are more concerned with their localities than with the nation. Special benefits for
special interests abound because *other* members are swayed by campaign contributions from the Political Action Committees associated
with those interests.

   Second, Congress's own procedures are inadequate to overcome
these difficulties. Seniority, partisan bickering, complex parliamentary
maneuvering, and powerful committees all serve to magnify the difficulties endemic in the institution. Were procedures in place to control
the narrow perspectives of most members and thereby to harness their
energies in pursuit of the national interest, Congress would be a much
better institution.

   Given that explanation of congressional dysfunction, one would
think the content of local editorials greatly resembles the content of the
national press. The difference is in the emphasis in these editorials on
the efforts, contributions, and successes of good people in Congress,
such as the local representatives and home state Senators. The positive
outcomes can now be explained by reference to the good guys in white.
More importantly, because these editorials do highlight congressional
accomplishments made possible through the efforts of the very legislators local citizens had the foresight to elect, the message is that Congress can and does work. Even if legislation going through Congress is

often delayed, belayed, and sometimes waylaid, when the chips are down, Congress will do the right thing. And it doesn't hurt to have our local heroes in the front line fighting the good fight.

NOTES

1. "Lean Times for Greens," *Raleigh (North Carolina) News & Observer*, 1 October 1994.

2. "Senate Saboteur," *Fresno (California) Bee*, 3 October 1994, 6(B).

3. "Hero on the Hill," *Providence (Rhode Island) Journal*, 4 June 1994, 8(A).

4. "Balanced Budget," *Jackson (Mississippi) Clarion-Ledger*, 25 February 1994, 8(A).

5. "Buying Votes Is a Crime," *Albuquerque (New Mexico) Journal*, 4 May 1994, 10(A).

6. "Voters Need to Remember Health Care Chaos at Election," *Boise Idaho Statesman*, 15 August 1994.

7. "Sen. Mitchell Steps Down," *Fresno (California) Bee*, 8 March 1994, 4(B).

8. "Two Thumbs Up: Seat-belt Bill Passes; A Special Justice Withdraws," *Lexington (Kentucky) Herald-Leader*, 19 February 1994, 10(A).

9. "Notch 1 for Brady Law," *Albuquerque (New Mexico) Journal*, 26 June 1994, 2(B).

10. Gary C. Jacobson, *The Politics of Congressional Elections*, 4th ed. (New York: Longman, 1997). See also Gary C. Jacobson and Samuel Kernell, *Strategy and Choice in Congressional Elections* (New Haven, Conn.: Yale University Press, 1981).

11. David Vogler, *The Politics of Congress*, 6th ed. (Madison, Wis.: Brown and Benchmark Publishers, 1993), 12.

12. John Hibbing and Elizabeth Theiss-Morse, *Congress as Public Enemy* (Cambridge, Mass.: Cambridge University Press, 1995).

13. Richard F. Fenno Jr., "If, as Ralph Nader Says, Congress is 'The Broken Branch,' How Come We Love Our Congressmen So Much?" in *Congress and Change: Evolution and Reform*, ed. Norman J. Ornstein (New York: Praeger, 1975), 277–87.

14. See, among others, Barbara Hinckley, *Congressional Elections* (Washington, D.C.: Congressional Quarterly, 1978); Jacobson, *Politics of Congressional Elections*; and Albert D. Cover, "One Good Term Deserves Another: The Advantage of Incumbency in Congressional Elections," *American Journal of Political Science* 21, no. 3 (August 1977), 523–41.

15. Mark J. Rozell, "Press Coverage of Congress, 1946–92," in *Congress, the Press, and the Public*, eds. Thomas E. Mann and Norman J. Ornstein (Washington, D.C.: American Enterprise Institute and Brookings Institution, 1994), 59–129.

16. Hibbing and Theiss-Morse, *Congress as Public Enemy*.

17. "Endorsement: Return Trent Lott to the U.S. Senate," *Jackson (Mississippi) Clarion-Ledger*, 6 November 1994, 6(G).

18. "Congressional Choices," *Albany (New York) Times-Union*, 29 October 1994, 6(A).

19. "Congress: Bereuter for Ninth Term," *Lincoln (Nebraska) Journal*, 28 October 1994, 17.

20. "LaRocco Disqualifies Himself from Re-election to House," *Boise Idaho Statesman*, 1 November 1994.

21. "Tony Beilenson's Victory," *Fresno (California) Bee*, 30 April 1994, 6(B).

22. "Mandates Strain Localities," *Boise Idaho Statesman*, 6 July 1994.

23. "Earthquake?: Surely, Federal Agency Jests," *Lincoln (Nebraska) Journal*, 24 December 1994, 10.

24. "Talking Through a 'Cap,'" *Raleigh (North Carolina) News & Observer*, 11 September 1994.

25. "Helms Vents; We All Pay," *Raleigh (North Carolina) News & Observer*, 6 October 1994.

26. "North Carolina Senator Should Be Denied Position," *Albuquerque (New Mexico) Journal*, 27 November 1994, 2(B).

27. "Loose Senatorial Cannon," *Lexington (Kentucky) Herald-Leader*, 22 November 1994, 12(A).

28. "Thumbs Up and Down," *Lexington (Kentucky) Herald-Leader*, 26 November 1994, 18(A).

29. "Hastings's Haitian Solution," *Providence (Rhode Island) Journal*, 12 June 1994, 12(D).

30. "Go GATT 'em!" *Providence (Rhode Island) Journal*, 27 November 1994, 8(D).

31. "Senate Saboteur," *Fresno (California) Bee*, 2 October 1994, 6(B).

32. Matthew C. Moen and Gary W. Copeland, *The Contemporary Congress: A Bicameral Approach* (Belmont, Calif.: West/Wadsworth, 1999), 176.

33. Roger H. Davidson and Walter J. Oleszek, *Congress and Its Members*, 5th ed. (Washington, D.C.: Congressional Quarterly, 1996), 427.

34. "Change the House Debate Rules," *Albany (New York) Times-Union*, 25 March 1994, 10(A).

35. "A Lot Better Than No Debate," *Raleigh (North Carolina) News & Observer*, 21 March 1994.

36. "Voters Need to Remember Health Care Chaos at Election," *Boise Idaho Statesman*, 15 August 1994.

37. "A Clunker in the House," *Fresno (California) Bee*, 15 December 1994, 4(B).

38. "Awareness Can't Be Mandated," *Albuquerque (New Mexico) Journal*, 12 December 1994, 6(A).

39. "Biennial Budget Boring but Beneficial," *Lincoln (Nebraska) Journal*, 15 January 1994, 15.

40. "Congress' Porcine Projects," *Albuquerque (New Mexico) Journal*, 4 January 1994, 6(A).

41. "Waiting for Reform," *Raleigh (North Carolina) News & Observer*, 13 May 1994.

42. "Running with the PACs," *Raleigh (North Carolina) News & Observer*, 4 November 1994.

43. "The Senate Votes for Cynicism," *Albany (New York) Times Union*, 8 October 1994, 6(A).

44. "Quake," *Lansing (Michigan) State Journal*, 10 November 1994, 12(A).

45. "Nationwide, Voters Say No," *Fresno (California) Bee*, 10 November 1994, 6(B).

46. "Shakeup in Congress," *Albany (New York) Times Union*, 9 November 1994, 14(A).

47. Davidson and Oleszek, *Congress and Its Members*, 8.

48. "Health Care: Legislative Process Officially Begins," *Jackson (Mississippi) Clarion-Ledger*, 20 March 1994, 4(G).

49. "Better Health Care Possible," *Boise Idaho Statesman*, 19 May 1994, 7(A).

50. "Take Some of These," *Providence (Rhode Island) Journal*, 23 January 1994, 8(D).

51. "Health Care: Playing for Major Marbles," *Lincoln (Nebraska) Journal*, 29 June 1994, 19.

52. "Critical Hour for Health Reform," *Fresno (California) Bee*, 16 June 1994, 8(B).

53. "Dizzying: Health Care Creates a National Headache," *Lansing (Michigan) State Journal*, 15 August 1994, 4(A).

54. "Quit Stalling on Health Care," *Albany (New York) Times Union*, 18 August 1994, 12(A).

55. "Health Reform: Votes Will Decide Blame/Credit," *Jackson (Mississippi) Clarion-Ledger*, 28 September 1994, 10(A).

56. "In Step on Gun Control," *Fresno (California) Bee*, 8 May 1994, 6(B).

57. "Crime Bill: Local Leaders Went to D.C. to Push It," *Jackson (Mississippi) Clarion-Ledger*, 18 April 1994, 8(A).

58. "Leaders Should Address Specific Crime Issues," *Albuquerque (New Mexico) Journal*, 13 August 1994, 14(A).

59. "Sideswiping the Crime Bill," *Fresno (California) Bee*, 15 August 1994, 4(B).

60. "Dead Aim," *Lansing (Michigan) State Journal*, 16 August 1994, 4(A).

61. "This Crime Bill is Hollow," *Albany (New York) Times Union*, 11 August 1994, 10(A).

62. "To Preserve the Crime Bill," *Fresno (California) Bee*, 16 August 1994, 6(B).

63. "Crime Bill: It's Worth Two Sleepless Nights," *Lincoln (Nebraska) Journal*, 23 August 1994, 6.

64. "The Price of a Crime Bill," *Raleigh (North Carolina) News & Observer*, 17 August 1994.

65. "Christmas Tree with a Badge," *Providence (Rhode Island) Journal*, 18 August 1994, 19.

66. "A Tough-call Crime Bill," *Fresno (California) Bee*, 2 August 1994, 4(B).

67. "Buying Votes Is a Crime," quoting Steven Moore, Cato Institute, *Albuquerque (New Mexico) Journal*, 4 May 1994, 10(A).

68. "Death Penalty," *Jackson (Mississippi) Clarion-Ledger*, 18 August 1994, 14(A).

69. "Leaders Should Address Specific Crime Issues," *Albuquerque (New Mexico) Journal*, 13 August 1994, 14(A).

70. "Crime Bill Redux," *Albany (New York) Times Union*, 22 November 1994, 10(A).

71. "Crime Time Melodrama," *Lexington (Kentucky) Herald-Leader*, 26 August 1994, 12(A).

72. "Crime Bill," *Jackson (Mississippi) Clarion-Ledger*, 27 August 1994, 14(A).

73. "Crime Bill Better than Nothing," *Fresno (California) Bee*, 28 August 1994, 10(B).

74. "A Pretty Good Crime Bill," *Providence (Rhode Island) Journal*, 31 July 1994, 14(D).

75. "To Preserve the Crime Bill," *Fresno (California) Bee*, 16 August 1994, 6(B).

76. "Crime Bill Better than Nothing," *Fresno (California) Bee*.

77. "A Tough-call Crime Bill," *Fresno (California) Bee*.

78. "Christmas Tree with a Badge," *Providence (Rhode Island) Journal*.

79. Rozell, "Press Coverage of Congress," 59.

80. Davidson and Oleszek, *Congress and Its Members*, 10.

Chapter Four

The Primacy of the President

President Bill Clinton had been in office just about a year when the Whitewater scandal broke in early 1994. Few might remember that his presidential honeymoon had been curtailed by the issue of gays in the military and by problems some of his appointees had with paying Social Security taxes for their nannies. Few might recall the relatively uneventful first year of Clinton's term. But then Whitewater broke into the open, complete with special prosecutor and aspersions cast on both Clinton and his wife, Hillary, marking his presidency indelibly.

Whitewater aside, both domestic policy and foreign affairs called for presidential attention. Events abroad, from North Korea's experimentation with a nuclear weapons program and Serbia's attempt to control developments in Bosnia to Haitian General Raoul Cedras's taking and holding power to prevent democratic elections, forced themselves on Clinton's attention. As the *Boise Idaho Statesman* pointed out, "U.S. foreign policy needs to be guided by the strong hand of a president."[1] The press and the public alike expect the president to guide the ship of state in the treacherous waters of international politics.

Domestic policy was no less a challenge. We had already canvassed editorial responses to congressional maneuverings in regard both to Clinton's proposal reforming health care and to the crime bill in the previous chapter. Editors found occasion to hold Clinton's feet to the fire on these issues, too. Complicating the matter, however, is the simple fact that the president does not make domestic policy single-handedly.

Working with and through Congress is the method the Constitution prescribes and practical politics dictates. But expectations of strong leadership, leadership to which Congress will never bow and the kind of leadership a wise president will therefore never exercise, underlie editorial criticism of Clinton. When Clinton, for instance, suggested in July of 1994 that he might be amenable to a health-care plan that did not include universal coverage, the *Albany Times-Union* criticized him for "making a fuzzy position . . . even fuzzier" and urged Clinton to "break with the politics of confusion and tell us where he stands . . . once and for all."[2]

Whether it is domestic or foreign policy, a president cannot satisfy all constituents or segments of the public. The goal, the *Lexington Herald-Leader* suggested, was to win the support of at least a majority of the people. Recalling that Clinton was elected with a popular vote of 43 percent, the editors pointedly noted that Clinton's "first job as president was getting the support of at least another 7 percent of the citizenry. But if that occurred to Clinton, you'd never know it from his behavior."[3]

If Clinton had had a honeymoon with the press, it would have been over long before 1994. By January, editors in the local daily press across the nation did not automatically give him the benefit of the doubt. They no longer, if they ever did, gave greater weight to good intentions. They no longer had optimistic high hopes for what a new president with new ideas with a new team of advisors and officials could accomplish. Although they were not necessarily part of "the 'Hate Clinton' industry,"[4] neither were they always the cheerleaders for his fan club. The honeymoon was at most a faded memory; the "marriage" had its ups and downs.

THE MEDIA PRESIDENCY

In 1960, Clinton Rossiter identified what he called a "significant change . . . in the authority and structure of the Presidency": "the opening of new channels of communication through which he can mold and measure public opinion."[5] His prediction has come true. The president enjoys unrivaled access to the media, benefits (and suffers) from constant journalistic coverage, and basks in the limelight of network television. Doris Graber's data show that, from August 1994 through July 1995, the presidency garnered over four times as much network television news coverage as did Congress.[6]

Two main benefits of this extensive media attention accrue to the president. One is simply that the public views and continues to view the president as the most important office holder in the nation. By comparison, citizens barely notice governors, senators, speakers of the House, and majority leaders of the Senate. The second is that such access to the press enables a president to publicize his agenda,[7] attempt to set the parameters for debate on public issues, and claim credit for successes, deserved or not, that occur during his administration. Washington political news, for ill or good, centers on the White House. Presidents take full advantage.

However, heavy press coverage brings disadvantages as well. Given the president's prominence in the news, the public cannot be faulted for thinking that it is his responsibility to act—and to act successfully—whenever a crisis or a problem arises. The public, therefore, holds high expectations about presidential performance, whether he wields significant authority over an issue or not. Similarly, while a president can easily claim credit for a favorable resolution of a sticky situation, he cannot as easily escape blame for policy failures during his watch. Is the economy doing well? The president can claim credit. Is unemployment up? The president can hardly avoid criticism.

For some time, scholars have thought presidents to be more effective in attaining their goals if their approval ratings were high. In Kernell's words, presidents are "heavily dependent on their popularity for their leadership."[8] The president's concern extends beyond public approval for its own sake, commendable as that approval may be in a democratic society. Rather, high popularity increases the likelihood that other political leaders will respond as the president wishes. "Presidential favorability ratings," Delli Carpini and Keeter say, "serve as indicators to Congress as to whether he should be followed."[9] Although Richard Neustadt argues that a president's prestige with "Washingtonians" carries more weight than his popularity in the populace, he notes that "the prevalent impression of a President's public standing tends to set a tone and to define the limits of what Washingtonians do for him or do to him."[10] Edwards finds that, indeed, when a president enjoys higher approval ratings, his success in Congress increases. As a result, Edwards suggests that a president "should attempt to influence members of Congress indirectly by strengthening his support among the American people."[11] As he said elsewhere, "It is difficult for others who hold power to deny the legitimate demands of a president with public support."[12]

Jones sharply disagrees. "Public standing of presidents, as measured by public approval ratings," he argues, "is inexactly related to . . . effectiveness in working with Congress."[13] At best, he maintains, "a high approval rating is a reminder of the potential costs in opposing the president." However, "[m]embers of Congress will vary considerably in their individual calculation of the costs within their own states and districts of opposing a popular president."[14] Misciagno falls into the same camp; she "challenges the general view within presidential studies that the public, and appeals to the public, represents an ultimate sources of power for the president."[15] Maslin-Wicks reviewed the "quantitative literature" and concluded that the results showed "the president exercises influence in the legislative process only 'at the margins' or under certain circumstances."[16] Cohen et al. find little relationship between district-level measures of presidential approval and members' support for the president on roll-call votes.[17]

Nevertheless, presidents seem to act as if winning popular approval will help them in Congress—and with leading the nation generally. "Presidents believe that high public approval will enhance their chances of legislative success with Congress," Cohen and colleagues say.[18] "Whether successful or not," Edwards insists, "the president's efforts to build coalitions among the public are designed to assist building coalitions in Congress."[19] Canes-Wrone's work supports the notion that a president's personal popularity is unrelated to his success in getting budgetary policies adopted by Congress, but, significantly, she finds that a president's public appeals for support do yield favorable results.[20]

Kinsey and Chaffee, however, caution against drawing too strong a connection between media content and presidential approval ratings. Interpersonal "discussions about politics," they contend, may also influence public evaluations of presidential performance, "over and above political communication received via the media."[21] On the other hand, Schaefer found "editorial writers [to] have a bias toward popularity, treating presidents with higher approval ratings more favorably."[22] Presidents cannot be faulted for seeing their popularity connected to the task of winning media support.

Most presidents in fact pay close attention to their dealings with the media. The relationship that develops has sometimes been termed adversarial, but it can be more accurately depicted as symbiotic. According to Dodds and Rozell, "[a]lthough a positive cordial relationship with the press does not guarantee favorable coverage, White House efforts to accommodate journalists and tend to their needs can help a great deal."[23] While presidents seek "media coverage conducive to their personal, policy, and political interests,"[24] media choices about what events to report and how to report them affect and sometimes stymie presidential goals. White House attempts to "influence press coverage through the use of public and press relations techniques" may work, but "success is never guaranteed, and no set of techniques will yield the same results for different presidencies," contends Rozell.[25]

News management becomes a key objective. Timothy Cook notes that "presidents must devote ever more time to finding ways to get to [the public] indirectly, through the resources of the news media."[26] As a result, the presidency has come to be seen from the media-relations perspective: It is now the "Six O'Clock Presidency,"[27] the "President as Interpreter-in-Chief,"[28] or the "'Image Is Everything' Presidency."[29] *Going Public*[30] describes a president's job today as well as anything. "Today," Jeffrey Tulis says, "it is taken for granted that presidents have a *duty* to constantly defend themselves publicly, to promote policy initiatives nationwide, and to inspire the population. And for many, this presidential 'function' is not one duty among many, but rather the heart of the presidency—its essential task."[31]

Presidential relations with the media consist chiefly of interactions with the representatives of the national media, collectively the White House press corps. Their products—news stories—are published in papers such as the *New York Times*, aired on television network broadcasts such as ABC's "World News Tonight," and transmitted to other news outlets through services such as the Associated Press. Presidential efforts at news management focus on these journalists and their reporting.

Some presidents have attempted to bypass the national news media. President Reagan invited editors from smaller newspapers across the country to meet with him from time to time. Early in his term, reports Sidney Blumenthal, President Clinton paid little attention to the White House press corps; instead, his "staff attempt[ed] to tap every media outlet except the Washington correspondents."[32] Whether these efforts result in different news treatment in outlying media markets is hard to determine. For the most part, local news outlets rely on the national media for the news from Washington.

They do not rely on national media for their editorial commentary on the presidency, however. Local editors do not have to protect their reporters' access to White House news. They are relatively immune from the blandishments that the administration offers to Washington reporters. Individually, local editors' newspapers seem insignificant to the president's overall media goals. Collectively, however, their editorials may affect how a president is perceived in localities across the nation. The cumulative effect on local public opinion and on the thinking and choices of state officials and the area's members of Congress should not be dismissed as trivial.

DOING THE JOB

Since Wildavsky's seminal piece on "The Two Presidencies,"[33] scholars have distinguished between the president's actions in foreign affairs and those concerning domestic policy. Presidential preferences for acting in international politics, despite the larger stakes at risk—war and peace, for instance—can be readily explained. In foreign policy, a president controls decisionmaking. He has access to information Senators and House members do not have. He speaks for the nation as a whole toward the rest of the world, and citizens view him as acting internationally on their behalf. Arthur Vandenberg was not far off when he said that partisanship ends at the water's edge. Testing the "two presidencies" thesis, however, Conley found "few indications . . . that the basis for bipartisanship existed for Clinton in his first two years."[34]

In domestic policy matters, however, presidents must not only consult with Congress, the bureaucracy, and, frequently, state governments, but they must often defer to them as well. Presidents who want to reform welfare, rebuild the nation's infrastructure, or clean up the environment can do so only when Congress passes the requisite legislation. But Congress, elected by different constituencies, concerned with different interests, and committed to different priorities, may not go along. If Congress agrees with a president's proposal, it nevertheless puts its mark on it. Presidents sometimes have no choice but to accept congressional changes in their domestic program.

Two different dynamics are at play here, though they are mirror images of each other. In foreign policy, the president plays the leading role. If Congress or anyone else wants to affect the president's foreign policy choices, the most common method is to criticize. In domestic policy, on the other hand, the president may propose legislation, but then stands on the outside watching Congress act. His main public option (he has many others behind the scenes) is also to criticize.

These patterns, of course, reflect the Madisonian system, which requires cross-institutional cooperation despite differences in authority, goals, and responsibility (in the sense of having to answer to others). Shared legislative power in domestic affairs pits Congress against the president whenever they disagree. Each has substantial weapons at their disposal. Because of the president's authority in foreign policy, however, Congress is reduced to sniping at the president's flanks in that arena.[35]

The "political folklore," suggesting that the "presidency basks in the limelight of publicity . . . while Congress waits in the shadows,"[36] implies that the president can more successfully "go public" with his concerns than can the Congress. In conflict between the branches, the president's greater access to media, accompanied by the presidency's greater ability to speak with one voice, would lead us to expect that the president would be more successful in getting his point of view across.

One might then expect similar patterns in editorial commentary. In foreign policy matters, editors could choose to be supportive of the president as spokesman for the nation as a whole, while echoing criticisms on his choices emerging from Congress. In domestic policy, editors could choose to focus more commentary on the president's criticisms of Congress, while miscalculating the extent of the president's power in the legislative process, calling him to task for not shepherding his proposals through Congress more successfully.

Doing the job of president extends beyond making policy decisions. The president must select others for his staff, his cabinet, and other posts in his administration. The quality of those individuals, and their peccadilloes, guide others in judging the president. If one or more run afoul of the law or alienate important constituencies with ill-considered remarks, the president's reputation is on the line.

Other choices, current or past, may ultimately affect a president's job performance. The press loves to attach labels to the circumstances in which these choices are embedded, such as Watergate, the Iran-Contra affair, or Whitewater. These decisions can call a president's integrity and his judgment into question. Media content has the capacity, therefore, to influence how people view him and how congressional leaders, foreign officials, and even members of his own administration respond to him.

One would be wearing rose-colored glasses if one were to think that editors would leave controversy over presidential appointees and presidential scandals alone. Not only are reporters attracted to conflict as news, but ongoing developments lend themselves to journalistic narrative forms involving drama and, ultimately, resolution. As James David

Barber put it, "The reporter sets out not to find facts, but to find a story."[37] More to the point, "a reporter is on the lookout for stories that will lead to other stories."[38] Editors find such stories irresistible as well, given the opportunities they present to pontificate, to preach, to uphold honesty and decency, or to contrast good and evil.

THE EDITORIAL COMMENTARY

As demonstrated in chapter 2, the editorials examined here frequently dealt with the presidency. The primacy of presidential news over other political news had its parallel in editorial subject matter. Despite the local attractiveness of the members of Congress from the area the newspaper served, the president was generally likely to be the topic of discussion in editorials. "First in war, first in peace, first in the hearts of his countrymen," was said of George Washington. To that can be added, for President Clinton in 1994, "first in editorial commentary."

Virtually anything newsworthy affecting national politics and foreign policy in Washington in 1994 involved President Clinton. In the previous chapter, we noted the attention Congress paid to Clinton's health-care reform bill and to the crime bill for which both Congress and Clinton wanted to claim credit. Welfare reform and budgetary politics also orbited around Clinton's White House, with Congress exerting a strong gravitational pull as well. A long litany of foreign policy problems with which Clinton had to deal included democracy in Haiti, Serbian attacks in Bosnia, North Korea's development of nuclear weapons, and the usual concerns of Middle East tensions, relations with Russia, and human rights issues in China. Midterm congressional elections, with a Republican surprise victory, and the emergence of Whitewater as a potential presidential embarrassment added further opportunities for editorial commentary on the president.

Foreign Affairs

President Clinton emerged clearly as the dominant actor in foreign affairs from a reading of these editorials. However, editorial writers seemed ultimately uncomfortable with presidential pre-eminence in foreign policy. Although they supported presidential actions in principle, they gave more than lip service to the notion that presidents should consult widely, especially with Congress, rather than act unilaterally.

Editors viewed public and political support as essential elements of successful foreign policy. The commentary on U.S. involvement in Haiti serves as a clear example.

Lieutenant General Raoul Cedras, commander of the military junta that ruled Haiti since a 1991 coup, rescinded his agreement to permit the return of Jean-Bertrand Aristide, the former president whom Haitian voters had elected to office. The clash between military power and incipient democracy presented compelling drama. The boatloads of refugees leaving the island (Hispaniola) underlined the severity and the pathos of the situation. The White House considered action, mulled over various possibilities, rattled its sabers, negotiated publicly and privately, and finally sent the Marines in to remove the military junta. Cedras and his fellow officers could read the handwriting on the wall and agreed to leave Haiti at the last minute, while Marines were already at sea. Aristide returned, and Clinton and the U.S. claimed success for democratic peoples everywhere.

Editorial commentary was not uniformly complimentary. Early in the year, editors sought clarity and commitment from the Clinton administration. In May, *Providence Journal* editors rejected Clinton's proposed tightened economic blockade: the new policy "will be about as successful as previous ones," they said, in an editorial pointedly titled, "Today's Haitian Policy."[39] Three months later, *Albany Times Union* editors could say that "The Haiti policy of the Clinton administration has never been either consistent or effective."[40] *Boise Idaho Statesman* editors minced no words in its evaluation of the White House's early approach: "Unfortunately, the Clinton administration isn't given to strategic thinking. It has little talent and apparently no desire to look beyond any current crisis in foreign affairs." The paper's solution? Clinton should provide "a clear and firm policy."[41]

As the crisis progressed, a clearer U.S. policy emerged: the threat of invasion to depose the Cedras regime. Editors waffled; some accepted its inevitability and others opposed using military force. "Advice to President Clinton: Don't use a U.S. cannon to rid Haiti of its military dictator gnats,"[42] the *Albuquerque Journal* said from the beginning. Lincoln editors called on Clinton to "resist the ultimate easy answer: sending in the Marines."[43] Albany readers were told that military intervention does not seem the right approach," since "there really is almost no U.S. security interest at stake in Haiti."[44]

However, editors resigned to military action did not welcome it. "Clinton should at least look at other options short of invasion," argued the *Fresno Bee*.[45] In Providence, editors wondered about the aftermath of an invasion: "What then?" Clear goals might keep the nation from "a trek through a snake-infested swamp."[46] Calling invasion "a lamentable course," the *Lincoln Journal* "remains opposed to a U.S.-led invasion," convinced "that the crisis there will not be solved with a quick little three-day military operation."[47] The only paper to back invasion unequivocally was the *Lexington Herald-Leader*, whose editorial was headlined: "Yes, Invade Haiti: The Case Is Clear; the Cause Is Just."[48]

Editors argued for consultation with Congress before military intervention began. The *Albany Times Union* editors noted pointedly that Congress includes "some hands . . . who are considerably more experienced in foreign affairs than there evidently are in the White House."[49] "Clear It with Congress," urged a Providence editorial headline.[50] Albuquerque editors opposed any invasion "until Congress votes to commit American lives to the cause of Haitian democracy."[51] Fresno editors recognized Clinton's dilemma: he "might have done more to persuade Congress," but "Congress has [not] behaved with courage and consistency," noting that the parties had changed sides since Bush was faced with the need to act militarily in the Gulf in 1991.[52]

What saved Clinton and the military operation, of course, was the diplomatic mission led by former president Jimmy Carter. When Carter, Colin Powell, and Sam Nunn successfully negotiated the peaceful withdrawal of Cedras, the *Lincoln Journal* called it a "breakthrough,"[53] and the *Fresno Bee* termed it a "cause for relief."[54] Despite the mission's success, the terms of the agreement Carter reached with Cedras were too generous for the Albany editors to accept. The accord was "a boon for the military junta," because it laid the groundwork for a grant of amnesty. Now, the editors argued, "[t]he Clinton administration . . . [must] partially extricate itself from the deal."[55] The consensus, however, was that the trio of U.S. negotiators "deserve praise and thanks" for their work.[56]

As a whole, these editorial writers credited Bill Clinton with the success of the venture. "Triumph in Haiti," trumpeted one editorial headline, adding that the outcome "represents a victory of conscience and good sense for Bill Clinton."[57] The *Jackson Clarion-Ledger* editors urged citizens to "give the president his due. President Clinton succeeded where failure seemed almost a certainty."[58] And despite having "opposed a U.S. invasion of Haiti," the *Lincoln Journal* editorialists admitted that "the Clinton administration has achieved a foreign-policy success."[59] Nevertheless, some editors still felt Congress should have been more involved, even on its own initiative: "Congress should have asserted its constitutional authority to commit or refuse to commit U.S. troops to duty in Haiti," Albuquerque editors told their readers.[60] Clinton gets the credit, but editors would have preferred congressional involvement in the process.

Domestic Policy

Getting congressional approval for domestic policy initiatives lies at the heart of presidential activity on most issues that directly affect the public: crime, health care, education, welfare, and the like. The public expects the president to deal with these matters, and citizens will judge a president's performance in part on whether he can get Congress to enact good, solid, and, one hopes, effective laws. "[O]ne of the president's most important jobs is to keep Congress concentrated on his legislative program."[61]

We have already, in the previous chapter, explored editorial commentary on congressional responses to Clinton's health-care legislation and the crime bill for which both Clinton and Republicans in Congress claimed responsibility. Let us now look at the proposals to reform welfare, proposals that did not pass in 1994 but set the stage for a new federal welfare policy later.

Having made "ending welfare as we know it" a central plank in his election platform, President Clinton repeated his request to Congress for welfare reform in his 1994 State of the Union address. He followed that up with a legislative package to Congress in the middle of June. Congress did not pass it before the November elections. The electorate then put a Republican majority in charge of Congress, a majority energized by their "Contract with America," with welfare reform as a major element. The new Congress would have to deal with it beginning the following January.

Soon after Congress met in January, the *Fresno Bee* urged the administration to keep its promise to reform welfare. It saw health care and welfare reform as intertwined, presenting "an adroit president" with the opportunity to "leverage" support for welfare reform "into critical support for universal health coverage."[62] Editors, however, did not envisage a fiscal windfall; to the contrary, reform would require additional "spending for job training, child care, and the like," the *Raleigh News & Observer* editors noted. "The challenge will be for Clinton to make the case that welfare reform is a smart and humane investment."[63]

But how does this ??? w/ the seeming knowledge ??? disgust ??? the press in ??? ??

As a result, Clinton was "finding welfare reform . . . a trifle more complicated than his slogan made it out to be."[64]

The political complexities and ironies did not escape editors' comments. "[T]he greatest threat to the president's welfare program is . . . from congressional Democrats facing re-election,"[65] the *Clarion-Ledger* pointed out. And the *Fresno Bee* noted that Clinton's "sweeping changes" requiring welfare recipients to find work within two years have put "hard-right welfare critics, who once emphasized work over welfare," into the awkward position of insisting "that only illegitimacy matters" when deciding who should receive welfare assistance.[66]

What is striking about these editorials' commentaries, however, is how little emphasis—indeed, even mention—there is of the legislative process itself. It is almost as if editors believe that President Clinton's sending legislative proposals to reform welfare to the Hill is sufficient. Only when the *Fresno Bee* remarked on the difficulty some "Democratic leaders" expected in the Senate Finance and the House Ways and Means committees in dealing with both welfare reform and Clinton's health-care package did any editors give much weight to the complexities of the legislative process. The president proposes, and the Congress disposes, in the old phrase, does not apply. Instead, the editors seem to imply that the president proposes, and the Congress votes it up or down, depending on whether the proposal is fatally flawed or not. Such a stance gives the president a prominence in domestic policy making that rivals his pre-eminence in foreign policy.

THE PERSONAL PRESIDENCY[67]

Maintaining prestige and popularity amid political controversy challenges every president. "The Washingtonians who watch a President have more to think about than his professional reputation. They also have to think about his standing with the public outside Washington."[68] Developments that diminish the public's approval of a president decrease the likelihood that Washingtonians—and other political leaders—will take political risks on the president's behalf. Liberal Democrats supporting the president's welfare reform proposal, for instance, would indeed be running a political risk.

In 1994, President Clinton faced a major threat to his standing with the public: the Whitewater revelations. The allegations raised called Clinton's integrity into question and asked questions about his judgment. Were editors prepared to give Clinton the benefit of the doubt or were they ready to throw him to the wolves?

The affair stimulated extensive editorial comment. Nine of the ten newspapers, excluding only the *Lansing State Journal*, ran several editorials on Whitewater. At the beginning of the year, some comment was relatively mild: events "may be no more serious than a conflict of interest."[69] The *Fresno Bee* guessed that "there is very little chance that Bill Clinton would ever be ultimately charged with any criminal violation."[70] Others hinted at a deeper concern: "the Clintons don't appreciate the significance of the Whitewater scandal to this presidency."[71] Indeed, Clinton's seeming lack of cooperation and even some interference in the early investigation suggested to the Albany editors that "President Clinton and his advisors have given little reason to believe they understand . . . the importance"[72] of the inquiry.

Editors evinced greater concern about the significance of the affair over the course of the year, as indications emerged that the Clintons and the White House were less than forthcoming and may have attempted to influence the Whitewater investigation behind the scenes. "[I]t was wrong," the *Lincoln Journal* stated, "for White House officials to try to get a Treasury Department friend to keep a hand in the investigation."[73] More strongly, the *Providence Journal* is convinced that "Whitewater figures . . . have been notably reluctant to cooperate with investigators. . . . The truth is that, with each passing day, it becomes increasingly obvious that damage control . . . has been the order of the day."[74]

Two factors come out clearly in editors' discussions of Whitewater: partisanship and distraction. The *Fresno Bee* hoped that special counsel Robert Fiske would succeed in "lifting the issue out of the swamp of partisanship and ill will in which it has been bubbling."[75] Labeling the entire episode a "partisan sideshow," the *Albuquerque Journal* suggested that "Republicans can make political hay" out of the affair, especially if the special counsel "spades up dirt or even information the GOP can 'spin' into dirt."[76] When Paula Corbin Jones filed her sexual harassment lawsuit against the president, the *Raleigh News & Observer* was sure that "[t]hose behind the suit aren't pursuing it for the welfare of the Republic. . . . This is about getting Bill Clinton."[77]

More frequent were comments about the distraction the Whitewater matter posed for the administration and for Congress. "As long as this mess drags on," noted the *Boise Idaho Statesman*, "Congress and the president are virtually paralyzed on important issues like health care and deficit reduction."[78] If Clinton would simply provide the public with the information it needs on Whitewater, "[t]hen we can get on to the policy issues facing the nation,"[79] said the Providence editors. The *Albuquerque Journal* editors worried about the attention devoted to the whole issue: "Some of that energy could be more usefully directed at issues average taxpayers care about deeply, such as crime, health care, jobs."[80]

What about the effect on the presidency itself? No editor commented that an investigation of this sort has a salutary effect on the presidency, cleansing it, if you will, and thereby strengthening it. To the contrary, editors were concerned that public confidence in the presidency would be undermined, whether by Democrats defending Clinton by undermining congressional investigations ("they have contributed to the President's continuing decline in public esteem and so in his ability to govern effectively"),[81] or by Republicans, using Whitewater "to score political points against the Clintons," damaging, among other things, "the nation's respect for its leadership."[82] "The Whitewater charges," the Raleigh editors pointed out, "cloud the public sector. They go to the heart of the matter of the trust between governors and governed."[83]

Editors did not connect public support with the president's performance. Readers were implicitly discouraged from linking presidential popularity to legislative success. The idea that members of Congress would be less likely to pass the proposals of a wounded president, the idea that a president not under a cloud would be a more effective lobbyist for his own program in Congress—these notions were conspicuous by their absence. If Whitewater made passage of Clinton's proposals in welfare, health care, and crime less likely, it was not because he was less popular with the cloud of Whitewater over his head, but that Congress was distracted from its duties.

EDITORS' EVALUATION OF THE CLINTON PRESIDENCY

In editorials, journalists feel free explicitly to criticize and to assess. Comments that would be out of place in "objective journalism" appear normal and appropriate in the newspaper's opinion column. Over the course of 1994, editors occasionally passed judgment on the Clinton presidency, and the grades they assigned varied from paper to paper and from month to month.

As a whole, editors considered Clinton as doing relatively well. In reviewing 1993, the president's first year in office, the *Jackson Clarion-Ledger* focused its attention on campaign "promises kept and pending." Its conclusion: a year of "some misses and hits."[84] The Albuquerque editors called it a "bruising first year in office."[85] In New York, the Albany editors thought "Clinton's first year in office was marked by some considerable accomplishments—and a good deal of luck."[86] But 1994 was a long year, and these positive, although somewhat lukewarm, evaluations came down.

By the summer, with Clinton's legislative proposals bogged down in Congress, Whitewater investigations continuing to receive media coverage, and various and sundry crises popping up around the world, editors' evaluations were decidedly more negative. The president's attempts to find a compromise on health care that his critics in Congress would find acceptable led the *Albany Times-Union* to castigate him for yet another "flip-flop"; it called on him to "break with the politics of confusion and tell us where he stands . . . once and for all."[87] Providence readers were told that "various White House scandals . . . and a string of foreign policy blunders and miscues" may doom Democrats in November. The prospect is that "his presidency could slide slowly but inexorably to oblivion."[88]

The *Fresno Bee* raised the contrast between performance ("By almost any conventional measure, the country is better off than it has been in years.") and expectations to explain the anger of voters in the fall of 1994. In doing so, the editors rattled off a series of missteps, from scandal to foreign affairs to appointment snafus and being "too much in thrall to mindless environmental dogma and political correctness."[89]

When the Republicans scored an overwhelming electoral victory in the November elections, the political context for the White House changed drastically. When the president responded, editors criticized him roundly, especially in the Boise and Lexington papers. Chastising Clinton for a lack of "core beliefs," the *Herald-Leader* pointed out that "[a]n effective president—conservative, liberal, or centrist—must demonstrate some core beliefs and principles from which he never wavers." But "[n]o one changes directions faster than" Clinton.[90] The *Idaho Statesman* took up the point: "Bill Clinton has a principled stand on the issues? Oh, please, give us a break."[91]

The implicit evaluations editors gave Clinton over the course of the year, during their commentary on health care, welfare reform, foreign policy, and other matters, were tilted toward the positive side. In 1994, editors did not perceive Clinton as a very good president, but he was certainly seen as a capable chief executive with potential. As the *Bee* editors noted, "the scope of domestic reform in the first two years of the Clinton administration could exceed anything since the New Deal."[92]

CONCLUSION

This examination of editorial commentary in local daily newspapers reinforces the prevalent notion of the primacy of the president in the press. Washington inside the Beltway revolves around the president, his agenda, and his actions. Much media content arising there, sent nationwide through the services of wire services, major national newspapers, and network television broadcasts, treats most political news from the perspective of the occupant of the White House. Editorials reproduce that emphasis in their repeated commentary on presidential actions and policies.

As a consequence, even far from the capital, views of the president enter into local public discourse. Rather than being irrelevant to matters public officials, political activists, and attentive newspaper readers are interested in, the editors' choice to comment extensively on presidential affairs emphasizes the implicit message that the president and his actions are worth attending to, whether in Washington or in Jackson, Mississippi.

If presidential prestige or popularity makes a difference in his ability to do his job and attain his goals, then what editors say in these newspapers may influence how the public views him. "For most Americans, understanding the presidency occurs . . . through the daily reporting and commentary of the media," Dodds and Rozell point out. They add, "for the public, the image of the president *is* reality."[93] Because citizens themselves have little direct experience with the president, mediated news reports and commentary remain an important source for their evaluation of presidents.

The picture of the primacy of the president that emerges from these editorials can be most effectively brought into focus by noting the connection editors draw between Congress and the president. Consistent with the "two presidencies" thesis, editors discuss presidential-congressional relationships at least somewhat differently. Underlying this difference, however, is a commonality that clearly puts Congress in second place in the national political hierarchy.

In foreign affairs, discussion centers on implementation of policy. The role Congress should play is one generally supportive of the president. Congress should help, in other words, rather than act on its own. If the risks of military action in Haiti, for instance, are too great, Congress can let the president know. If the options the president seems to be exploring can lead to pitfalls, Congress can keep him from making mistakes. Congress can serve as an evaluation board for presidential actions in foreign policy. And Congress does so, but as individual members rather than as an institution. In this way, Congress can let the people speak through them.

In domestic policy, the emphasis of the editors' comments is more on the making of the policy than on its implementation. That is unsurprising in itself, since lawmaking deals more with setting up programs than with running them. Editors' expectations are that Congress would essentially validate presidential proposals; if Congress finds problems with the president's proposals, it should fix them, if possible. Here Congress is depicted less as worrying about how the president's policy would work as it is with whether the policy should be adopted in the first place, and if so in what form. Because legislation has to be adopted, if at all, by institutional action, the emphasis here is more on the collective decisionmaking in the two chambers.

Nevertheless, more important than this minor difference is an overriding consistency, one that reinforces the notion that the president is the dominant political actor in the nation, from the editors' perspective. That commonality is that in both areas, editors see Congress as playing a decidedly secondary role, with their main purpose being to find and expose mistakes in the president's proposals. The president's domestic legislative program sets the agenda for Congress as much as his initiative in foreign policy sets the stage there.

Both foreign and domestic policy questions in 1994 presented editors with controversy about basic priorities in the nation. Military intervention overseas and overhaul of health care and welfare, for instance, center at the core on inescapable value questions. Editors tended to treat Clinton lightly on these points, with little value-centered criticism. Perhaps that reflected "Clinton's passionate centrism."[94] Perhaps it reflected their recognition that Clinton was addressing the issues that most of the public wanted the government to address. Whatever the reason, 1994 was not a year of editorials highly critical of the president.

Even in terms of Whitewater, the editors were more concerned with process—bringing the information forward—than they were with criticism of the president. They certainly voiced their doubts, but the editorials by and large did not undermine either the president's popularity or his reputation with the public. The assumption about Whitewater all along was that the whole affair was relatively minor, it involved the president's action before he took office, and it could be cleared up relatively quickly when all the information was available. In the meantime, editors deferred judgment.

But neither did they go out of their way to praise Clinton. One searches quite diligently to find editorials devoted chiefly to praising Clinton. When one occurs, it usually reflects Clinton acting as Head of State, such as the editorials commenting on the president's speech on the fiftieth anniversary of D-Day in Normandy, France.

The overall image coming out of these editorials, then, is of a president with some potential, dealing with significant problems, who has made mistakes and can benefit from the guidance and criticism of Congress in avoiding future missteps. But the steps are clearly the president's to take; Congress and others form a supporting cast in the political drama starring the president.

NOTES

1. "Congress Can't Fill Policy Void," *Boise Idaho Statesman*, 10 June 1994.
2. "Mr. Clinton's Rocky Course," *Albany (New York) Times-Union*, 27 July 1994, 10(A).
3. "Landslide Mentality," *Lexington (Kentucky) Herald-Leader*, 11 November 1994, 12(A).
4. "The 'Hate Clinton' Industry," *Raleigh (North Carolina) News & Observer*, 25 July 1994.
5. Clinton Rossiter, *The American Presidency*, rev. ed (New York: Harcourt, Brace & World, 1960), 110, 114.
6. Doris A. Graber, *Mass Media and American Politics*, 5th ed. (Washington, D.C.: Congressional Quarterly, 1997), 271.
7. The president's ability to focus other policymakers' attention to political issues, "a precursor to agenda setting," may not be as powerful as originally thought. Edwards and Wood call their findings on "the ability of the president to set the agenda of Congress and the media . . . mixed." George C. Edwards III and B. Dan Wood, "Who Influences Whom? The President, Congress, and the Media," *American Political Science Review* 93, no. 2 (June 1999): 327, 341.
8. Samuel Kernell, *Going Public: New Strategies of Presidential Leadership* (Washington, D.C.: Congressional Quarterly, 1986), 173.

9. Michael X. Delli Carpini and Scott Keeter, *What Americans Know about Politics and Why It Matters* (New Haven, Conn.: Yale University Press, 1996), 58.

10. Richard E. Neustadt, *Presidential Power and the Modern Presidents: The Politics of Leadership from Roosevelt to Reagan* (New York: Free Press, 1990), 74.

11. George C. Edwards III, *Presidential Influence in Congress* (San Francisco: W. H. Freeman, 1980), 109.

12. George C. Edwards III, "Building Coalitions," *Presidential Studies Quarterly* 30, no. 1 (March 2000): 48.

13. Charles O. Jones, *The Presidency in a Separated System* (Washington, D.C.: Brookings Institution, 1994), 283.

14. Jones, *The Presidency*, 119.

15. Patricia S. Misciagno, "Rethinking the Mythic Presidency," *Political Communication* 13, no. 3 (July/September 1996): 329.

16. Kimberly Maslin-Wicks, "Two Types of Presidential Influence in Congress," *Presidential Studies Quarterly* 28, no. 1 (winter 1998), 108.

17. Jeffrey E. Cohen, Jon R. Bond, Richard Fleisher, and John A. Hamman, "State-Level Presidential Approval and Senatorial Support," *Legislative Studies Quarterly* 25, no. 4 (November 2000), 577–90.

18. Cohen, et al., "State-Level Presidential Approval and Senatorial Support," 577.

19. Edwards, "Building Coalitions," 58.

20. Brandice Canes-Wrone, "The President's Legislative Influence from Public Appeals," *American Journal of Political Science* 45, no. 2 (April 2001): 313–29.

21. Dennis F. Kinsey and Steven H. Chaffee, "Communication Behavior and Presidential Approval: The Decline of George Bush," *Political Communication* 13, no. 3 (July/September 1996): 289.

22. Todd M. Schaefer, "Persuading the Persuaders: Presidential Speeches and Editorial Opinion," *Political Communication* 14 (January/March 1997): 108.

23. Graham G. Dodds and Mark J. Rozell, "The Press and the Presidency: Then and Now," in Philip G. Henderson, ed., *The Presidency: Then and Now* (Lanham, Md.: Rowman & Littlefield, 2000), 160.

24. David Paletz, *The Media in American Politics: Contents and Consequences* (New York: Longman, 1999), 240.

25. Mark J. Rozell, "Presidential Image-Makers on the Limits of Spin Control," *Presidential Studies Quarterly* 25, no. 1 (winter 1995): 68.

26. Timothy Cook, *Governing with the News: The News Media as a Political Institution* (Chicago: University of Chicago Press, 1998), 131.

27. Frederick T. Smoller, *The Six O'Clock Presidency: A Theory of Presidential Press Relations in the Age of Television* (New York: Praeger, 1990).

28. Mary E. Stuckey, *The President as Interpreter-in-Chief* (Chatham, N.J.: Chatham House Publishers, 1991).

29. Richard Waterman and Gerald Wright, *The "Image is Everything" Presidency* (Boulder, Colo.: Westview Press, 1999).

30. Kernell, *Going Public*.

31. Jeffrey K. Tulis, *The Rhetorical Presidency* (Princeton, N.J.: Princeton University Press, 1987), 4.

32. Sidney Blumenthal, "Letter from Washington: The Syndicated Presidency," *New Yorker*, 5 April 1993, 44.

33. Aaron Wildavsky, "The Two Presidencies," *Trans-Action* 4, no. 2 (December 1966): 7–14.

34. Richard S. Conley, "Unified Government, the Two Presidencies Thesis, and Presidential Support in the Senate: An Analysis of President Clinton's First Two Years," *Presidential Studies Quarterly* 27, no. 1 (spring 1997): 244.

35. See *U.S. v. Curtiss-Wright Export Corp.*, 299 U.S. 304 (1936).

36. Graber, *Mass Media and American Democracy*, 288.

37. James David Barber, "Characters in the Campaign: The Literary Problem," in *Race for the Presidency: The Media and the Nominating Process*, ed. James David Barber (Englewood Cliffs, N.J.: Prentice-Hall, 1978), 114.

38. Barber, "Characters in the Campaign," 117 (italics omitted).

39. "Today's Haitian Policy," *Providence (Rhode Island) Journal*, 10 May 1994, 14(A).

40. "Back to Square One," *Albany (New York) Times-Union*, 25 August 1994, 12(A).

41. "Bringing Change to Haiti Calls for Clear, Firm Policy," *Boise Idaho Statesman*, 2 June 1994.

42. "Leave Haiti to OAS," *Albuquerque (New Mexico) Journal*, 14 April 1994, 14(A).

43. "Bad Voodoo: U.S. Troops Invading Haiti," *Lincoln (Nebraska) Journal*, 24 May 1994, 10.

44. "Don't Invade Haiti," *Albany (New York) Times-Union*, 5 August 1994, 12(A).

45. "The Junta Thumbs Its Nose," *Fresno (California) Bee*, 14 July 1994, 6(B).

46. "Invade, and Then What?" *Providence (Rhode Island) Journal*, 15 July 1994, 12(A).

47. "Invasion: Voodoo Foreign Policy," *Lincoln (Nebraska) Journal*, 16 September 1994, 18.

48. "Yes, Invade Haiti: The Case Is Clear; the Cause Is Just," *Lexington (Kentucky) Herald-Leader*, 16 September 1994, 10(A).

49. "Let Congress in on Haiti," *Albany (New York) Times-Union*, 13 September 1994, 6(A).

50. "Clear It with Congress," *Providence (Rhode Island) Journal*, 14 September 1994, 12(A).

51. "Congress Should Join Haitian Invasion Debate," *Albuquerque (New Mexico) Journal*, 15 September 1994, 12(A).

52. "Point of No Return," *Fresno (California) Bee*, 17 September 1994, 6(B).

53. "Haiti: A Breakthrough for Two Presidents," *Lincoln (Nebraska) Journal*, 19 September 1994, 6.

54. "Power and Persuasion," *Fresno (California) Bee*, 20 September 1994, 6(B).

55. "Unravel the Haiti Deal," *Albany (New York) Times-Union*, 28 September 1994, 12(A).

56. "Perils Await U.S. in Volatile Haiti," *Albuquerque (New Mexico) Journal*, 20 September 1994, 10(A).

57. "Triumph in Haiti," *Raleigh (North Carolina) News & Observer*, 20 September 1994.

58. "Haiti: A Foreign Policy Success for Clinton," *Jackson (Mississippi) Clarion-Ledger*, 12 October 1994, 8(A).

59. "Haiti: Now Comes the Hard Part," *Lincoln (Nebraska) Journal*, 13 October 1994, 12.

60. "Two Wrongs Don't Make a Right," *Albuquerque (New Mexico) Journal*, 10 October 1994, 8(A).

61. Edwards, *Presidential Influence*, 117.

62. "Don't Delay Welfare Reform," *Fresno (California) Bee*, 10 January 1994, 6(B).

63. "Welfare as an Investment," *Raleigh (North Carolina) News & Observer*, 24 March 1994.

64. "Welfare Reform, a Step at a Time," *Albany (New York) Times-Union*, 12 March 1994, 6(A).

65. "Welfare Reform," *Jackson (Mississippi) Clarion-Ledger*, 14 June 1994, 10(A).

66. "A Welfare 'Stepping Stone,'" *Fresno (California) Bee*, 17 June 1994, 8(B).

67. The term is adapted from Theodore Lowi, *The Personal President* (Ithaca, N.Y.: Cornell University Press, 1985).

68. Neustadt, *Presidential Power*, 73.

69. "Whitewater: White House Should Be Open Book," *Lincoln (Nebraska) Journal*, 7 March 1994, 4.

70. "The Whitewater Questions," *Fresno (California) Bee*, 5 January 1994, 6(B).

71. "A Special Counsel," *Providence (Rhode Island) Journal*, 15 January 1994, 12(A).

72. "Reality Time for Mr. Clinton," *Albany (New York) Times-Union*, 8 March 1994, 10(A).

73. "Whitewater: Words Better Left Unsaid," *Lincoln (Nebraska) Journal*, 28 July 1994, 16.

74. "Whitewater Whitewash," *Providence (Rhode Island) Journal*, 3 August 1994, 10(A).

75. "Fiske's Progress," *Fresno (California) Bee*, 6 July 1994, 6(B).

76. "Partisan Sideshow," *Albuquerque (New Mexico) Journal*, 17 January 1994, 8(A).

77. "Behind Clinton's Crisis," *Raleigh (North Carolina) News & Observer*, 7 May 1994.

78. "Lead, Don't Follow the Herd," *Boise Idaho Statesman*, 18 March 1994, 11(A).

79. "Fine Performance," *Providence (Rhode Island) Journal*, 26 March 1994, 10(A).

80. "Playing the Market," *Albuquerque (New Mexico) Journal*, 31 March 1994, 16(A).

81. "Whitewater Whitewash," *Providence (Rhode Island) Journal*, 3 August 1994, 10(A).

82. "Frothing over Whitewater," *Fresno (California) Bee*, 29 July 1994, 4(B).

83. "Stonewalling Whitewater," *Raleigh (North Carolina) News & Observer*, 8 January 1994.

84. "Clinton," *Jackson (Mississippi) Clarion-Ledger*, 23 January 1994.

85. "Fasten Your Seatbelts," *Albuquerque (New Mexico) Journal*, 27 January 1994, 16(A).

86. "Bill Clinton: A New Moderate," *Albany (New York) Times-Union*, 26 January 1994, 10(A).

87. "Mr. Clinton's Rocky Course," *Albany (New York) Times-Union*, 27 July 1994, 10(A).

88. "He Needs Another Comeback," *Providence (Rhode Island) Journal*, 2 June 1994, 10(A).

89. "Why So Angry?" *Fresno (California) Bee*, 5 October 1994, 6(B).

90. "Presidency on a Slippery Slope," *Lexington (Kentucky) Herald-Leader*, 20 November 1994, 1(E).

91. "Clinton Spins in Political Winds," *Boise Idaho Statesman*, 14 December 1994.

92. "Moving on the Domestic Agenda," *Fresno (California) Bee*, 1 April 1994, 4(B).

93. Dodds and Rozell, "The Press and the Presidency," 160.

94. "Clinton's Passionate Centrism," *Fresno (California) Bee*, 27 January 1994, 6(B).

Chapter Five

Blame the Bureaucrats

For generations, public and politicians have railed against shortsighted, misguided, and bloated bureaucracies in Washington. Former Alabama Governor George Wallace used to refer to decisionmakers in the various agencies comprising the executive branch as "pointy-headed bureaucrats." Stories about the number of regulations one agency or another issued to control cabbage growing or pickles for hamburgers reinforced images of people in Washington out of touch with the real world making life miserable for everyone else. Legends persist that only by filing form after form—in triplicate, at least—can one prove compliance with bureaucratic regulations.

Editors share this image of bureaucracy. The *Lincoln Journal* scoffed when the General Services Administration required the federal office building in downtown Lincoln, Nebraska, to be made earthquake proof, even though "Lincoln has not felt tremors that did much more than jiggle the crockery since 1877."[1] Editors at the *Fresno Bee* railed at the absurdity of the U.S. Department of Agriculture allowing frozen chickens to be labeled fresh: "How long can such nonsense remain frozen in law?"[2] A "Catch 22" problem in complying with Immigration and Naturalization Service regulations (employers were required to provide truthful information for which they could not ask their employees) led the *Boise Idaho Statesman* to charge that the agency was "making criminals of honest Americans."[3] Editors think no more kindly of the federal bureaucracy than they do of Congress.

POLITICS AND ADMINISTRATION

These negative views result in part from the decidedly awkward and almost untenable position the federal bureaucracy occupies in the political system. While agencies are charged with administering policy, they have limited authority to adjust those policies to prevent problems. Bureaucrats must administer programs fairly, which usually means uniformly across the nation, even when circumstances differ. When a federal department performs well, the White House takes credit; when it performs poorly, the agency must take the blame. The bureaucracy is, in the public mind at least, separate from politics, but its actions generate significant political effects. Under the president's nominal control, the bureaucracy seems to respond more to clientele groups than to the occupant of the White House.

Although bureaucracies fit awkwardly into the U.S. system of representative democracy, they nevertheless form a significant component of the national government. They represent the element of government people are most likely to come into contact with. The Post Office delivers the mail, the National Weather Service provides forecasts, and the Social Security Administration sends out checks. The negative images of bureaucracy do not automatically extend to the transactions people have with such agencies. Goodsell reports that most citizens evaluate the bureaucracies they deal with rather favorably.[4] Not only do people think they were treated well and properly, but generally they were also satisfied with they way the agencies handled their complaints when problems did arise. In most day-to-day dealings with the bureaucracy, people think well of government agencies. As Cook puts it, "when government bureaucrats serv[e] people's wants and needs, as is usually the case in close, specific, client-oriented encounters, public administration wins positive public judgments."[5]

The negative judgments about bureaucracies arise, it seems, more out of the impressions the public forms about the operation of the administrative apparatus of government generally. Cook suggests that "the impact [administrative agencies] have on public policy" presents a perspective that "violates basic expectations" people hold.[6] That contrast between expectations and reality arises out of the disjunction between what programs are intended to do (e.g., maintain air quality), and what they accomplish (e.g., mounds of paperwork and expensive testing).

Bureaucracies may not be able to overcome that gap in expectations. For an agency to adapt a policy, for instance, to every locality may require more information than it has. So testing for certain pollutants in drinking water makes sense for most locations but becomes inappropriate in areas where those pollutants rarely occur. But agency personnel may have no way of knowing enough about each of the circumstances where their regulations are going to be applied to make exceptions or may not have the authority to exempt some localities from general requirements.[7] As a consequence, bureaucracies wind up requiring people, businesses, and local governments to take sometimes onerous actions that will have no effect on the problem the program is designed to alleviate.

These patterns make people unsure about whose interests agencies pursue. It is a question of responsiveness. To whom is the bureaucracy accountable? On one level, an easy answer for the public is, 'to no one,' since bureaucrats working with Civil Service protection enjoy considerable job security. On a deeper level, the answer is more complex. Agency personnel are accountable to Congress, to the president, to the public, and to the specific clientele they serve. Scholz and Wood, for instance, found that "political responsiveness" helped explain variation in the probability that the Internal Revenue Service would audit a taxpayer's return.[8] However, these groups frequently have conflicting goals. The conclusion citizens draw is that agencies are less concerned with the public good or the difficulties their regulations cause than they are with protecting their power and their clienteles.

Agencies develop "political alliances" which results in "a style of policy making that emphasizes minority interests and muffles . . . majoritarian interests."[9] With such clientele politics, agencies become spokesmen for special interests, as has happened with the Department of Education and teachers and the Federal Aviation Administration and the airlines, to cite just two examples. Agencies' concern with the public interest is then easily questioned. "Red tape" and various delays inherent in any large administrative agency become simply evidence of a reluctance on the part of the bureaucracy to act expeditiously in the national interest.

No matter, then, how satisfactory citizens' personal contacts with the bureaucracy are, the overall impression of governmental agencies being slow and unresponsive, imposing burdensome requirements, and working to protect special interests even at the cost of the public good overwhelms the positives. But if it is not personal experience that accounts for public opinion on the bureaucracy, then the source must be elsewhere. Could it be media coverage?

BUREAUCRACIES IN THE MEDIA

Media attention to the federal bureaucracy is sporadic at best. In part, this pattern reflects the needs of the agencies involved and therefore how readily they make news available to reporters. Paletz points out that "departments vary considerably in their desire and need for media coverage."[10] "Some agencies, such as those responsible for consumer protection," says Stephen Hess, "need attention; others may consider publicity counterproductive to their mission, as CIA director William Casey concluded when he eliminated his agency's separate press operation."[11]

Agencies that welcome media coverage run larger press operations, issue more press releases, and make it easier for journalists to find and report the news emanating from the agency. The purpose? "To keep Congress and the public informed about the good they and their programs are doing."[12] Agencies that find media coverage intrusive at worst and useless at best devote few resources to helping reporters cover their work.

Studies of news coverage of the bureaucracy are relatively rare. Hess's work cited above, one of the most insightful on the nexus between press and agency, includes the bureaucracy–news media interaction as part of a larger study exploring reporters and government officials in Washington generally. As journalists do themselves, he devotes more attention to the White House and to Capitol Hill than to agencies that comprise the executive branch. David Morgan, in his study of government press information officers (PIOs), notes significant differences between the more visible and the less visible agencies.[13] His study, however, is so centered on the activities of the PIOs and their relationships with reporters that the overall pattern of agency press coverage does not emerge.

As a consequence, political communication scholars know comparatively little about media coverage of the bureaucracy. It is clear that beat assignments and general newsworthiness will affect whether news stories are filed and used. We lack, however, the degree of specificity about attempts to influence content, to "manage the news," or to use media coverage as a political tool that we have in our knowledge of White House and Capitol Hill news operations.

One can then only speculate about the tone and content of news regarding the federal bureaucracy. Three suppositions seem appropriate.[14] First, stories about failures and conflict—or "a notable success"[15]—arising out of agency actions will appear often. The Forest Service, for instance, probably received more coverage in the spring of 2000 after its "controlled burn" around Los Alamos, New Mexico, devastated the area than it did in several previous years combined. Second, news about the actions of the more familiar governmental agencies (e.g., the Environmental Protection Agency and the Social Security Administration) or a well-known official (such as C. Everett Koop or James Watt) will be reported more frequently than news from more obscure agencies. Finally, agencies whose actions affect the market area of the news outlet in question will be in the news more than other agencies.

These three suppositions may indeed reinforce each other. A failure by a well-known agency affecting a local area will generate even more substantial news coverage because it combines all three factors. All other things being equal, the more newsworthy a story, the more prominence and space a newspaper will give it. The most prominent news stories about federal agencies that average readers are likely to come across in their local papers will then dramatize the agencies' shortcomings, mismanagement, and disregard for what should have been done.

As discussed in chapter 2, if one of the factors that leads editors to choose one topic for commentary over another is newsworthiness, then one would expect editorial commentary to reinforce these perceptions with critical comment.

Are there reasons for editors to comment favorably on federal agencies? Yes. When an agency successfully accomplishes a mission or steps back from a mistake it has made, one would expect editors to respond favorably. Positive comments, however, presented as exceptions to a generally negative pattern, do little to challenge perceptions of problems and bureaucratic mismanagement generally.

EDITORIAL COMMENTARY

Editors of the daily newspapers examined in this work devoted considerable attention to the workings of the federal bureaucracy, although they wrote more often about Congress and the president. As expected, their commentary centered on various dissatisfactions with agency decisions or agency actions. Actions by the Environmental Protection Agency, the Immigration and Naturalization Service, the Forest Service, the Department of Agriculture, and the Department of Defense bore the brunt of most editorial criticism. The Departments of Commerce, Labor, State, and Transportation were virtually invisible in these editorials.

When agency actions affected local concerns, editors responded. When agency actions offended editorial sensibilities, editors took up their pens. When agency leaders transgressed ethical boundaries, editors took to the pulpit. Occasionally, successes stimulated editorial commentary, but rarely so. Editorial attention was reserved for the bureaucracy's mistakes and missteps, thereby reinforcing the public's image of problems and ineptitude that has plagued governmental agencies for decades.

Local Concerns and Bureaucratic Action

Few concerns are more local in nature than the condition of the land and the water in an area. The Environmental Protection Agency (EPA), charged with maintaining the quality of the environment, ran into some editorial roadblocks in 1994 when its regulations or proposed regulations collided head-on with local conditions.

Safe drinking water represented one of those issues. The EPA proposed limits for radon in drinking water of around 200 picocuries per liter. In New Mexico, where naturally occurring radon concentrations reach over 2,000 picocuries per liter, meeting the EPA's standards "could cost New Mexico communities hundreds of millions of dollars." Calling it a "ridiculously stringent standard," the *Albuquerque Journal* editors called for "a dose of common sense and proportion" that "the federal government too often lacks."[16] The *Lincoln Journal* similarly objected to an EPA water monitoring requirement "for hundreds of substances that may or may not be present and may or may not be harmful," suggesting that it be postponed "until [communities] found a foolish Swiss banker or a buried treasure big enough to pay for it."[17]

Procedures the EPA uses get a lot of criticism. The EPA's air quality proposals for California, for instance, were "drawn up in Michigan by consultants who have had little or no contact with California," who, according to the *Fresno Bee*, "thought Sacramento was a suburb of Los Angeles."[18] The *Raleigh News & Observer* charged the EPA with failing to sponsor "research to supply [the] facts" about the right way to protect the "coastal plain ecosystem." The problem, the paper noted, was that the EPA is "treating the likes of Weyerhaeuser Co. as if they were pioneers in buckskins instead of corporate timber behemoths."[19] What many people would consider typical bureaucratic bungling was the subject for a rare *Lansing State Journal* editorial about national issues: the EPA "threatened to fine about 900 small water systems in Michigan for neglecting to file drinking water test results." In fact, the reports were submitted, but the EPA lost them. "Unbelievable," the paper said; the situation "must have taxpayers rolling their eyes with frustration as they watch another federal bureaucracy in action."[20]

Boise Idaho Statesman editors voiced several concerns about the bureaucracy's management of wilderness areas around the state. They opposed Forest Service proposals to limit jet boats on the Snake River in the Hells Canyon area, calling it "unfair" to restrict access until "the land, water quality, fishery and wildlife" would be hurt, but not before.[21] But editors were pleased with the "U.S. Fish and Wildlife Service's sensible reintroduction plan" to bring the gray wolf back to the Idaho wilds.[22] They also applauded the Forest Service's "eminently sensible approach" for forest preservation, providing "the timber industry with a reasonable supply of trees to cut down, while ending the destructive management practices of the past."[23] The paper kept a watchful eye on wasteful spending, though: it sharply criticized the expenditure of $70,000 on a "ski playground" outside Yellowstone Park for the use of park employees, calling it "an arrogant misuse of public funds."[24]

Similar examples from almost any one newspaper could be developed, where local concerns affected by the national bureaucracy generate editorial comment. The *Albuquerque Journal* published five editorials in five weeks about the Interior Department's policies in managing federal grasslands, concerned about what effect proposed increases in grazing fees would have on ranchers in New Mexico. "It would be unconscionable for the Democrats in Santa Fe and their fellow Democrat from Arizona [Interior Secretary Bruce Babbitt] by way of Washington to collaborate in rewriting the grazing rules without hearing from and considering . . . the needs of the people who have lived here for generations."[25]

One could readily write an editorial on almost any subject from the perspective of these local newspapers: "Although the agency has lofty goals in mind that we all appreciate and value, it suffers from major difficulties in reaching the right decision. The right decision for this area means taking into account what makes us different. The agency has not done so, and as a consequence, it will cause more problems than it will solve. If it would rid itself of its bureaucratic blinders, it would recognize that the proper decision is the one we are suggesting here."

Whether it is the impact on North Carolina tobacco farmers of the Food and Drug Administration's declaration that nicotine is addictive[26] or the difficulties Nebraska farmers would have if their new pickup trucks had less power in order to meet Department of Transportation fuel economy standards,[27] the argument is the same. The bureaucracy has failed to adequately understand and therefore to address the real problems people face.

The National Bureaucracy

Editors' responses to actions taken by agencies in the federal bureaucracy understandably dealt with a large variety of issues, from immigration and milk additives to the metric system and school lunches, reflecting the range of concerns addressed by federal programs of one sort or another. Although these issues affect their readers as well as the rest of the nation, local readers were affected no more than anyone else was. Editors therefore had no particular local interests to speak for or defend. As a result, their commentary departed from the pattern we identified in the previous section.

Generally, editors criticized bureaucratic actions. For the most part, the criticism contrasted agency decisions with basic values. The release of the report detailing Federal Bureau of Investigation actions in the Ruby Ridge affair resulting in the deaths of two people led the *Albany Times-Union* to charge the FBI with running "roughshod over the lives of citizens."[28] The FBI, it said, "should not be in the business of executing suspected criminals in the field."

Less dramatically, the *Providence Journal* disagreed with the Food and Drug Administration's refusal to require that milk from cows treated with a synthetic growth hormone that increases milk production be labeled as such. Labeling would let people themselves "decide which risks they find acceptable"; otherwise, "the government wrongly deprives citizens of this important choice."[29] The *Lincoln Journal* and the *Albany Times-Union* sided with the Providence paper. Lincoln editors insisted that if consumers "want the information, they should get the information. . . . Their government should not stand in their way."[30] Albany editors bluntly asked, "why should consumers trust the government . . . on this matter? It's not as if the government has not counseled us falsely in the past on health matters."[31]

These examples illustrate the extent to which editors view the results of bureaucratic decisionmaking skeptically. Not only does it reach results too frequently inconsistent with basic principles of this society, but it is slow and cumbersome. The Federal Aviation Administration's work is a case in point, according to the *Fresno Bee*: "A cumbersome risk benefit analysis process has delayed implementation of safety reforms that have long been regarded as cost effective."[32] In hyperbolic fashion, the *Albuquerque Journal* described the EPA's Superfund caustically: "as fast and effective in restoring the nation's worst toxic waste sites as Superman cleaning up an illegal kryptonite dump."[33]

One would think that a slow process would enable agencies to reach results consistent with shared values. According to the editors, that does not happen. When the Commission on Immigration Reform proposed that a national identity card be issued to everyone as a way of combating illegal immigration and its accompanying problem, the hiring of undocumented aliens, several newspapers jumped on the idea. Providence readers learned that the proposal "has the potential for the invasion of privacy . . . Big Brother and all that."[34] The *Times-Union* in Albany compared it to "an internal identity card of the kinds that had become so infamous in Europe at one time."[35] When an agency withdraws a proposed rule that would, if implemented, conflict with underlying civic principles, editors applaud. For instance, the *Jackson Clarion-Ledger* pronounced it "the wise thing" to do when the Equal Employment Opportunity Commission decided not to implement a guideline dealing with religious expression in the workplace. The editors' rationale? "It is not the business of the federal government to decide what is proper religious expression and what is not."[36]

Surprisingly, relatively few editorials lambasted federal agencies for stereotypical bureaucratic bungling. Several, however, fit the pattern. Lexington editors gave a "thumbs down" to the EPA for granting $500,000 to Utah State University for "rounding up cattle and fitting them with a device that will measure the amount of methane released when a cow belches."[37] Raleigh editors labeled the building of a new facility for the National Reconnaissance Office a "marble-clad $304 million megaboondoggle." Calling it "a child of Cold War . . . secrecy-paranoia," the paper decried the use of federal funds for "exterior marble from Italy and Norway [and] a racquetball court as well as aerobics and locker rooms."[38] When the Internal Revenue Service printed a half million income tax forms in Spanish and only 718 had been used and submitted by May, the *Providence Journal* gave "the IRS credit for at least trying," but it called the targeting of non-English-speaking populations "dubious." People showed "those well-intentioned IRS officials what an ordinary taxpayer could have told them in a minute: In a country where 327 languages are spoken, it makes sense to concentrate on English."[39]

When agencies do something right, however, editors make note of that, too. Both the *Albuquerque Journal* and the *Raleigh News & Observer* applauded the Department of Agriculture's proposed new standards for lower-fat school lunches, even though the changes won't be met with "cheers in the lunchroom."[40] Parents should support the "long overdue" changes and "yank" school lunches "out of the past and into the present."[41] When the Food and Drug Administration, "after years of pressure from consumer and health groups," adopted new seafood safety rules, the *Fresno Bee* said consumers would no longer be "playing roulette with the fish course" in their meals.[42] The Jackson editors liked the Women, Infants and Children program (it "works for Mississippi's babies") and urged the state's representatives in Congress to protect it.[43] "The reduction in Mississippi's infant mortality rate," they pointed out, "can be directly attributed to the WIC program."

To achieve objectives the editors agree with, they are ready to compromise what would in other contexts be overriding values. Regulating secondhand smoke, for instance, which involves "even more government intrusiveness in the lives of Americans," is nonetheless acceptable compared to "the potential lives saved."[44] Despite the lack of a "clear indication of a disease burden" caused by dioxin contamination, the Albany editors want the EPA to "err on the side of caution" and to "begin curtailing those activities that result in the production of dioxins."[45] Even that usual bugaboo, too much regulation, can be swept aside if the goal is worth it: Meeting the requirements of new EPA landfill regulations may be "expensive," and involve a "lot of federal regualation [*sic*]," but "those regulations are very much valid and very much needed" to ensure "safer and cleaner drinking water."[46]

Problem Children

For the most part, federal bureaucrats are faceless, nameless, anonymous people. Rarely does an editorial mention one by name, with two exceptions. When heads of cabinet-level departments take an action deserving comment, the editors will usually refer to them specifically. There is nothing noteworthy here. But when a lapse in judgment occurs, editors name names and fire when ready. These missteps can be readily explained and therefore avoided, editors suggest. Officials have lost touch with basic values and have begun to think of themselves as special. At the same time, officials need to realize that they have a greater responsibility to adhere to higher standards than the rest of us. They are, after all, the public's servants. Or so the editors would have us think.

In late 1994, President Clinton fired Surgeon General Joycelyn Elders when her blunt remarks, especially about masturbation, made her a liability to his administration. Seven newspapers explained the departure, all but one agreeing that "she was increasingly ham-handed, and her clumsy brand of candor became a luxury the Clinton administration could no longer afford."[47] She, according to the editors, lacked the "subtle touch. She got her points across with a sledgehammer,"[48] and she "broached serious and sensitive subjects without seeming to recognize their seriousness and sensitivity."[49] "Good riddance!" exclaimed the Jackson editors. "Her opinions were far too extreme for average Americans to stomach."[50] Her "bumptious public statements . . . all of which seemed designed to give maximum offense"[51] were indicative of the fact that she "never grasped the fact that the opinions of the surgeon general . . . carried the weight of the office."[52] In the opinion of the editors, it was not simply her statements but her failure to recognize the higher standards an officeholder has to meet.

The exception? The *Lincoln Journal* editors thought that "President Clinton [had] been looking for a reason to fire" her, and "apparently decided he had found one."[53] Only the Providence editors agreed that "the White House had been looking for a reason to fire her,"[54] but none but the Nebraska editors thought her actions did not warrant her dismissal.

An ethical cloud hung over Agriculture Secretary Mike Espy after disclosures that he had accepted gratuities from food processors whose plants his department inspected. After a period of denying that the gifts had influenced his decisions, Espy resigned his office. This incident presented the stereotypical case bureaucracy-haters love to cite: special favors from special interest groups perhaps influencing officials' decisions, and the officials in question bending their ethics at the expense of the public interest.

Editorial criticism ran true to form. The *Albany Times-Union* called it "a wake-up alarm about the ethical conduct" of Clinton appointees.[55] Lincoln readers were told that Espy "failed to keep proper distance between regulating agency and regulated interest" and that "his moral compass," if he will "get it functioning . . . is pointing toward the door."[56] Only Espy's home state *Jackson Clarion-Ledger* was restrained in its criticism when the story broke. "Espy," it said, "showed poor

judgment. . . . He should have known better."[57] But, it said three weeks
later, "accepting gifts and campaign contributions from special interests
is enshrined" in Congress. "Shouldn't Congress . . . be on the same
footing regarding ethics?"[58]

By the time Espy resigned, the *Raleigh News & Observer* agreed
with their Jackson counterparts about the disparity between the ethical
standards acceptable in Congress and those applied to the bureaucracy.
Members of Congress, the paper pointed out, "countenance the very behavior that cost Espy his job."[59] Both Albany and Lincoln editors re-
gretted the need for the resignation: Espy was "once a promising public servant with a strong record of accomplishment,"[60] said the
Times-Union, and the Lincoln *Journal* praised him for having
"launched some commendable policy initiatives."[61] The *Albuquerque
Journal* noted that the White House should share the blame for having
"failed to establish and enforce the high ethical standards it promised
for presidential appointees."[62]

The arrest and conviction of Aldrich Ames for spying for the Soviet
Union and Russia while working for the Central Intelligence Agency
also stimulated a burst of editorials critical of the federal bureaucracy.
Although the papers generally deplored Ames's treason, which led to
the execution of at least ten Russians working undercover for the CIA,
the main thrust of the editorials were aimed at the CIA itself, not the
mole. How could the CIA have failed "to discover the spy in its head-
quarters?"[63] "The far more important matter" than Ames's duplicity, the
Albany editors said, was "how it was possible for a CIA officer with top
secret clearance to have peddled such sensitive information for so long
without having been found out."[64] "Any overworked narc working for
a small county sheriff's department could have done better" than the
CIA, said the *Fresno Bee*.[65]

Editors used the incident as an opportunity to criticize the CIA and to
imply that greater oversight of this agency was sorely needed. The *Bee*
questioned "the agency's own internal security practices" and raised the
"more basic" concern: "the poor performance of U.S. intelligence concerning a range of major events, from predicting Saddam Hussein's invasion of Kuwait in 1990 to understanding the fragile state of the Soviet economy in the years preceding the Soviet Union's collapse."[66]
Albany editors agreed: "the agency has failed almost every important
test of intelligence gathering put to it."[67]

The Ames matter "may just shove Congress over the edge into real
oversight"[68] of the CIA, the editors of the Albuquerque paper hoped.

"[A] complete restructuring" is needed, Albany editors argued, "so that Congress has greater day to day oversight over what the CIA is up to."[69] "It's obvious," said the *Raleigh News & Observer*, "that the agency needs streamlining and refocusing," so that it no longer functions "in an absence of full public accountability."[70]

CONCLUSION

Far from being invisible, the federal bureaucracy appears frequently in local daily newspaper editorials. Most agency personnel, however, would no doubt prefer the commentary be more positive. Although one should not characterize the editorials dealing with federal administrative agencies as uniformly negative, criticism and disagreement appear much more often. This pattern resembles the tone of news coverage generally, with journalists seemingly judging negative news more newsworthy. Occasional complementary discussion finds its way into the editorials, but not enough to affect one's overall impression.

Editors showed little hesitation in reinforcing stereotypes of the bureaucracy. Mismanagement, wasteful spending, ethical lapses, and just plain incompetence stimulated editorial responses regularly. If readers thought federal agencies were out of touch with the world they lived in, editorial commentary would back that idea up. If readers felt that bureaucrats were more concerned with special interests than with doing what was right for the nation, editorials provided examples. If readers worried that their tax dollars were not being put to good use, editors told them they had good cause to worry.

The year 1994 saw neither massive bureaucratic scandals of the scope and magnitude of the Housing and Urban Development controversy during the Reagan administration, nor such quiescence that federal agencies did not show up on reporters' radar screens. The pattern of the editorial commentary found in this canvass, therefore, likely typifies the content of editorials over time.

By devoting as much editorial commentary to the federal bureaucracy as the papers did, the editors subtly emphasized to their readers the importance and relevance of these administrative agencies to their lives. However, editors' choice of topics highlighted offices such as the EPA, the CIA, INS, and the Forest Service. Regulations and restrictions emerging from the EPA, INS, OSHA, and other such agencies stimulate comment, while the actions of many other governmental departments pass unnoted. The image of the federal bureaucracy thus generated is one of an intrusive government regulating for its own sake.

By contrast, editors rarely devoted much space to agencies' success. Agencies that adopted regulations to protect the public received little if any credit. Offices that successfully accomplished their goals did so without notice. Editors provided no counterweight to the heavy emphasis on bureaucratic ineptitude and mistakes. Even though editors frequently admitted that agency officials were acting conscientiously and in good faith, editors still criticized their actions. Success, the normal outcome, did not reach the editorial columns—not enough controversy there.

Bureaucrats were generally anonymous. With the exception of well-known agency personnel (e.g., Attorney General Janet Reno), editorials rarely mentioned individual officials by name. The mistakes editors called to readers' attention were caused by someone holding some position in the bureaucracy. By keeping bureaucrats anonymous, editors reinforced the conception of a giant organization where real people and real interests get lost. Keeping them nameless also implied that the problem lay in the structure itself, not in the people who staff it.

The criticisms embodied in the editorials carried an implicit validation of basic societal values. An individual's right to choose, for instance, outweighed bureaucratic convenience. Efficiency was worthwhile, but not if it involved a restriction on privacy. Not only did the criticisms, then, reinforce the consensual societal values editors identified with, but they also quietly distinguished the good people who read the local paper from the bureaucrats in Washington who just did not get it. The underlying theme that these contrasts between agency actions and widely shared values demonstrated was that government personnel are indeed out of touch with what is important and right.

Unfortunately, as the survey of the editorials showed, editors did not stick to that position. When editors liked proposals for governmental action, then a conflict with basic values can be accommodated. Then, a restriction on choice may be worth it; then, an increase in regulations may be a small price to pay. To put it differently, referring to basic values in criticizing agency actions is a strategic choice. When the outcomes seem more desirable, however, strategy calls for flexibility, even when strongly held values come into play.

Attentive readers of these editorials would, over the course of the year, recognize the extensive impact of executive branch actions on their lives. They would have, however, little reason to change how they view the bureaucracy, nor would they have any reason to disagree with Ronald Reagan's famous aphorism: "government isn't the solution; government is the problem."

NOTES

1. "Earthquake?: Surely, Federal Agency Jests," *Lincoln (Nebraska) Journal*, 26 December 1994, 10.

2. "Icy Hand of Bureaucracy," *Fresno (California) Bee*, 24 December 1994, 6(B).

3. "Crazy Immigration Rules Unduly Burden Employers," *Boise Idaho Statesman*, 20 June 1994.

4. Charles T. Goodsell, *The Case for Bureaucracy: A Public Administration Polemic*, 3rd ed. (Chatham, N.J.: Chatham House, 1994), esp. ch. 2.

5. Brian J. Cook, *Bureaucracy and Self-Government: Reconsidering the Role of Public Administration in American Politics* (Baltimore, Md.: Johns Hopkins University Press, 1996), 3.

6. Cook, *Bureaucracy and Self-Government*, 3.

7. For an examination of a policy which allows bureaucrats to use their discretion to reflect state differences, see Lael R. Keiser and Joe Soss, "With Good Cause: Bureaucratic Discretion and the Politics of Child Support Enforcement," *American Journal of Political Science* 42, no. 4 (October 1998): 1133–56.

8. John T. Scholz and B. Dan Wood, "Controlling the IRS: Principals, Principles, and Public Administration," *American Journal of Political Science* 42, no. 1 (January 1998), 141–62.

9. Jack H. Knott and Gary J. Miller, *Reforming Bureaucracy: The Politics of Institutional Choice* (Englewood Cliffs, N.J.: Prentice-Hall, 1987), 124, 133.

10. David Paletz, *The Media in American Politics: Contents and Consequences* (New York: Longman, 1999), 264.

11. Stephen Hess, *The Government/Press Connection: Press Officers and their Offices* (Washington, D.C.: Brookings Institution, 1984), 101.

12. Randall B. Ripley and Grace A. Franklin, *Congress, the Bureaucracy, and Public Policy*, 3rd ed. (Homewood, Ill.: Dorsey Press, 1984), 96.

13. David Morgan, *The Flacks of Washington: Government Information and the Public Agenda* (Westport, Conn.: Greenwood Press, 1986).

14. These suppositions are based on conventional conceptions of "newsworthiness." For two lists of factors that comprise newsworthiness, see Doris A. Graber, *Mass Media and American Politics*, 5th ed. (Washington, D.C.: Congressional Quarterly, 1997), 106–8, and Jan Pons Vermeer, *"For Immediate Release": Candidate Press Releases in American Political Campaigns* (Westport, Conn.: Greenwood Press, 1982), 17–18.

15. Paletz, *The Media in American Politics*, 265.

16. "Don't Impose Stringent Radon Limits for Water," *Albuquerque (New Mexico) Journal*, 31 July 1994, 2(B).

17. "Drinking Water: Testy about Testing," *Lincoln (Nebraska) Journal*, 16 October 1994, 12(B).

18. "Wrong Turn on Air Quality," *Fresno (California) Bee*, 5 August 1994, 6(B).

19. "Not Swamped with Facts," *Raleigh (North Carolina) News & Observer*, 3 February 1994.

20. "Leaky: EPA Water Reporting Defies Explanation," *Lansing (Michigan) State Journal*, 23 July 1994, 4(A).

21. "Hells Canyon for Everyone," *Boise Idaho Statesman*, 7 July 1994.

22. "Wolf Reintroduction Plan Good Compromise for Idaho," *Boise Idaho Statesman*, 23 November 1994.

23. "Forest Ripe for Policy Change," *Boise Idaho Statesman*, 14 December 1994.

24. "Decision $70,000 Too Late," *Boise Idaho Statesman*, 4 November 1994.

25. "Hear All the Voices, " *Albuquerque (New Mexico) Journal*, 23 January 1994, 2(B).

26. "Tobacco Woes Are Real," *Raleigh (North Carolina) News & Observer*, 4 August 1994.

27. "Pickups: A Power Trip," *Lincoln (Nebraska) Journal*, 13 September 1994, 8.

28. "Questionable Tactics," *Albany (New York) Times-Union*, 25 December 1994, 4(B).

29. "This Milk Needs Labeling," *Providence (Rhode Island) Journal*, 6 February 1994, 10(D).

30. "Milk Hormone: Consumers Entitled to Labeling," *Lincoln (Nebraska) Journal*, 17 February 1994, 16.

31. "Tell Us What's in our Milk," *Albany (New York) Times-Union*, 28 February 1994, 6(A).

32. "How Safe Is Air Travel?" *Fresno (California) Bee*, 22 December 1994, 8(B).

33. "Superfund Super-Snafu." *Albuquerque (New Mexico) Journal*, 7 February 1994, 6(A).

34. "A National I.D. Card," *Providence (Rhode Island) Journal*, 5 August 1994, 12(A).

35. "We Don't Need National ID," *Albany (New York) Times-Union*, 17 November 1994, 12(A).

36. "Harassment: Forget Rule for Religious Harassment," *Jackson (Mississippi) Clarion-Ledger*, 22 September 1994, 10(A).

37. "Ups and Downs: Beaver Hits Middle Age; Methane Matters," *Lexington (Kentucky) Herald-Leader*, 4 June 1994, A(12).

38. "Here's What They Hate," *Raleigh (North Carolina) News & Observer*, 14 November 1994.

39. "IRS's Bilingual Flop," *Providence (Rhode Island) Journal*, 9 September 1994, 12(A).

40. "When the Carrot Sticks Fit," *Raleigh (North Carolina) News & Observer*, 25 June 1994.

41. "Get the Fat Out," *Albuquerque (New Mexico) Journal*, 18 July 1994, 6(A).

42. "Better Odds on Seafood," *Fresno (California) Bee*, 25 January 1994, 4(B).

43. "WIC: Mississippi Need This Vital Program," *Jackson (Mississippi) Clarion-Ledger*, 25 November 1994, 14(A).

44. "Clearing the Smoke," *Albuquerque (New Mexico) Journal*, 10 February 1994, 16(A).

45. "The Danger of Dioxin," *Albany (New York) Times-Union*, 17 September 1994, 6(A).

46. "Garbage: New Regulations Costly but Needed," *Jackson (Mississippi) Clarion-Ledger*, 11 April 1994, 6(A).

47. "Elders' Exit," *Fresno (California) Bee*, 13 December 1994, 4(B).

48. "Dr. Elders' Verbal Hemorrhages," *Albany (New York) Times-Union*, 13 December 1994, 18(A).

49. "Elders' Fire too Hot," *Raleigh (North Carolina) News & Observer*, 13 December 1994.

50. "Elders: Loose Cannon Clinton Could Ill Afford," *Jackson (Mississippi) Clarion-Ledger*, 13 December 1994, 10(A).

51. "Elders' Nonmedical Leave," *Providence (Rhode Island) Journal*, 13 December 1994, 12(A).

52. "Elders' Brash Mouth Led to Her Removal," *Albuquerque (New Mexico) Journal*, 15 December 1994, 20(A).

53. "Joycelyn Elders: Victim of Damage Control," *Lincoln (Nebraska) Journal*, 13 December 1994, 6.

54. "Elders' Nonmedical Leave."

55. "Spies and Mr. Espy," *Albany (New York) Times-Union*, 14 August 1994, 4(E).

56. "Espy: Choose Door Marked 'Exit,'" *Lincoln (Nebraska) Journal*, 17 August 1994, 16.

57. "Espy: Example Telling, but Charges Weak," *Jackson (Mississippi) Clarion-Ledger*, 10 August 1994, 8(A).

58. "Espy: Criticism Bounced Back to Congress," *Jackson (Mississippi) Clarion-Ledger*, 30 August 1994, 8(A).

59. "From Espy to Lobby Reform," *Raleigh (North Carolina) News & Observer*, 7 October 1994.

60. "Mr. Espy's Tattered Credibility," *Albany (New York) Times-Union*, 5 October 1994, 12(A).

61. "Agriculture: Time for a Fresh Face," *Lincoln (Nebraska) Journal*, 5 October 1994, 14.

62. "Secretary of Agriculture Not Only One to Blame," *Albuquerque (New Mexico) Journal*, 5 October 1994, 10(A).

63. "A Bizarre Tale of Greed," *Lexington (Kentucky) Herald-Leader*, 26 February 1994, 10(A).

64. "Fix the CIA," *Albany (New York) Times-Union*, 1 March 1994, 14(A).

65. "The Keystone Spooks," *Fresno (California) Bee*, 5 March 1994, 4(B).

66. "The Questions after Ames," *Fresno (California) Bee*, 2 May 1994, 6(B).

67. "The CIA Needs Watching," *Albany (New York) Times-Union*, 16 August 1994, 10(A).

68. "Ames Affair May Spark Congress to Rethink CIA," *Albuquerque (New Mexico) Journal*, 3 October 1994, 6(A).

69. "Clean House at the CIA," *Albany (New York) Times-Union*, 13 November 1994, 4(B).

70. "Smarter with Intelligence," *Raleigh (North Carolina) News & Observer*, 30 December 1994.

Chapter Six

Judges in Black Robes

Winston Churchill was referring to the Soviet Union in his famous aphorism calling it "a riddle wrapped in a mystery inside an enigma." For most Americans, the phrase can be aptly applied to the United States Supreme Court. The riddle asks how the Court affects citizens; the enigma is how the Court can be both political and judicial; the mystery is what happens behind its closed doors. Lacking the visibility of the presidency, shrouding its disagreements and decisions in esoteric legal terminology, the Supreme Court is easily the most distant, least approachable, and least understood of the three branches of the national government.

Perhaps by design, the Supreme Court is an awe-inspiring institution. The justices wear black robes, sit behind a massive high desk during court sessions, and conduct the rest of their business behind closed doors. They grant few interviews. They do not solicit outside support for their individual—or the Court's institutional—positions. Other than in the confusingly labeled "opinions" deciding the cases, they do not explain their thinking or justify their positions. It is as if an oracle consults omens to determine whether an action should be permitted or not and announces its conclusion in a way that only the initiated can understand. No wonder scholars refer to the "cult of the robe."

Editorial commentary can serve to explain the Court to readers. Editors, not constrained by the need to report the news in an inverted pyramid style, can use their columns to help the public make sense out of the

Court's pronouncements. Using cues such as ideology, editors are able to place the results of litigation before the Court in a larger political context. Using specific circumstances surrounding local and state concerns, editors may relate the Court's decisions to matters affecting their readers directly. In explaining the Court, editors ultimately reinforce its image as a mysterious body whose positions govern future political action.

THE COURT AND ITS DECISIONS

The judiciary's main function, similar to that of other branches of government, is to resolve conflicts. It does so by applying legal principles, devising new ones if necessary, to the dispute between the litigants before the bench. Lower courts spend most of their time considering cases involving no complex questions of law. The U.S. Supreme Court, however, devotes its attention almost exclusively to cases where statutes, precedents, or Constitution offer no clear guidance. Many of these cases directly or indirectly entail policy considerations that go beyond the interests of the parties to the case. In that way, the Supreme Court serves to resolve conflicts in the political arena, much as a law passed by Congress, a regulation issued by the bureaucracy, or an executive order emanating from the White House might.

Despite the similarity in impact on policy among the branches, the Supreme Court is unique in the sense that only it must offer a justification for its decision, and it must base that justification on principles of law, principles that it, because of *stare decisis*, is bound to follow in the future. Whereas members of Congress can defend a vote by citing district interests at stake, and whereas the president can explain a decision to deploy troops by citing the national interest, the Court cannot account for its positions with explicit references to policy concerns.

Because no appeal can be taken from Supreme Court decisions, its interpretation of what the Constitution requires is in some sense final. Therefore, the Court has the special opportunity to instruct the nation as to the meaning of the Constitution. In Funston's words, the Court "perform[s] as a national seminar in political theory."[1] In applying constitutional principles to the cases before it, "the Court will detail the underlying principles of American government and teach the people of the larger, philosophic ramifications of their acts."[2]

Funston correctly does not argue that the Constitution dictates specific outcomes; the document in its many ambiguities allows for a range of interpretations. Efforts by scholars to explain Justices' use of their discretion in constitutional interpretation have centered on the attitudinal model, whose most prominent practitioners today are Segal and Spaeth.[3] Boiled down to its essence, the attitudinal model suggests that Justices' backgrounds, preferences, and ideologies affect how they respond to the ambiguous cues cases present. Therefore, Justices hearing the same arguments, reading the same briefs, and applying the same Constitution will respond differently. How a case is decided, then, depends on who sits on the Court as well as on the issues involved. As the editors of the *Albuquerque Journal* put it, "The Constitution and the law contain the same words no matter who reads them, but their application to the infinite variety of human conditions is what brings them to life."[4]

Attempts both to influence Court decisions (many interest groups will file *amici curiae* briefs) and to explain the outcomes rely in large part on the attitudinal model. Briefs and oral argument by counsel will focus on the "swing votes" perceived to be crucial to winning the case and tailor their points to appeal to those Justices' predilections. News reports call the public's attention to what journalists perceive to be voting blocs on the Court. The notion that Justices may disagree because they approach cases from differing perspectives is now widely shared.

The Supreme Court's interpretation of the Constitution sets the parameters for political action by coordinate branches, as well as by states and lower courts. The source and justification for their decisions, therefore, become matters of concern to political actors from presidents to leaders of interest groups and local officials. May a school permit a student to lead a prayer over the public address system before the next home football game? The Supreme Court's answer to the question—and its reasons for that answer—guides legislators, activists, and school board members alike in setting, influencing, and implementing future policy. When the Court has spoken, its pronouncements on the meaning of the Constitution usually carry the day.

They carry the day, however, because of voluntary compliance. Lower court judges choose to apply Supreme Court precedents (instead of, for instance, routinely distinguishing away their relevance). State officials adjust their policies, so that any resulting litigation from their actions would not be overturned. Federal officials no longer apply regulations and laws that the Supreme Court has determined to run counter to constitutional provisions. Although we can all point to counterexamples (responses to the school desegregation case[5] quickly come to

mind), most Supreme Court decisions encounter only minor roadblocks
on the way to their implementation.

Such voluntary compliance rests heavily on public support for the
Court and its work. Caldeira points out that "the United States Supreme
Court must depend to an extraordinary extent on the confidence . . . of
the public."[6] However, "popular support for the Supreme Court is limited."[7] Caldeira and Gibson find that "broad political values," rather
than "support for specific policies," are more closely related to support
for the Court.[8] Hoekstra, furthermore, found that public support varied
based on people's responses to specific Court decisions with which they
were familiar.[9] The Court cannot simply count, then, on a reservoir of
support that would automatically lead to voluntary compliance on the
part of officials and public alike.

NEWS COVERAGE OF THE SUPREME COURT

Murphy and Pritchett rightly point out that "In order to comply with a
Supreme Court ruling, officials and interest groups must know that the
ruling has been issued and be able to understand it."[10] Johnson and
Canon put it in the form of a question: "Do the potential consumers of
a judicial policy know of the policy?"[11] Of course, the litigants to a case
are informed of the Court's decision and what is required of them by the
Court directly (or indirectly through counsel). It is the broader popula-
tion, those who must make decisions over subjects about which the
Court has now spoken, who may or may not know that the Supreme
Court has acted and what it has said.

What they know is problematic. Substantial research over the past
several decades leads on to the conclusion that news coverage of the
Supreme Court is sketchy, inaccurate, and incomplete. Whether in
daily newspapers,[12] in newsmagazines,[13] or on television,[14] the consensus finding is that "decisions . . . covered by the press tend to be reported briefly and sketchily, particularly by network news and non-
elite daily newspapers."[15] It would be safe to conclude, if these studies
present an accurate picture of the state of Supreme Court reporting,
that most policymakers have little clear idea what the Court requires of
them, if anything.[16] Compliance with Supreme Court decisions on the
part of the consuming population presupposes clearer knowledge of
Court actions than most of them can regularly expect from routine
news coverage.

Reporting of decisions varies from outlet to outlet. Although the Associated Press "is committed to covering most Supreme Court decisions,"[17] most newspapers choose among the cases to report ones they find most newsworthy.[18] When reported, "stories rarely advance beyond a description of the outcome of the decision. Typically, they do not expand to other critical tasks, such as explaining the decision process, placing the decision in the context of other decisions, and reporting reactions."[19] The late Justice Lewis F. Powell Jr., had no qualms about the lack of publicity surrounding the Court's actual decision-making: "this unstructured and informal process . . . simply cannot take place in public."[20]

Other than stories about the decisions the Court hands down, news coverage is sporadic. When a controversial case is scheduled for oral argument, some stories may appear in the press. Reporters have few sources of information for news stories about the Court. Most of their stories, therefore, tend to build on information available at or around the Supreme Court itself. Spokespersons for interest groups wanting to share their perspectives, for instance, make themselves available to the Court press corps. Davis reports that "interest groups are pleading for the opportunity to serve as sources."[21]

In contrast to the highly politicized news coverage the media accord Congress and the president, "most coverage" of the Supreme Court, Paletz says, "still adheres to the myth of judicial exception: the assumption that the Supreme Court is above and beyond politics."[22] The end product is then more deferential and respectful, and perhaps conducive to building public support for the Court, than news stories about the other branches of government.

Because of the density of Supreme Court opinions, the lack of press releases to aid journalists in understanding and conveying the thrust of Court decisions, and the difficulty in translating complex legal terminology into language comprehensible to the public, news stories do not necessarily help citizens grasp the import of the latest Court pronouncement. Perhaps editorials can play a role in helping readers make sense of the actions the Supreme Court has taken.

EXPLAINING THE COURT

Editorials present journalists with an opportunity to explain Supreme Court behavior. Free from the constraints of objectivity, editors may range more freely than news reporters in providing background and context for Supreme Court actions. In doing so, editors may put specific cases into a pattern, connecting a current decision with previous ones. Editors may also relate the Court's actions to state and local concerns, pointing out how today's resolution of a case before the Court is likely to affect policy matters being taken up in the market the paper serves.

One can see in three areas the effort editors make to account for the Supreme Court's actions. First, editors' use of ideological labels in describing both opinions and Justices gives readers a guide for attributing meaning to the outcomes. Second, the editors' assessments as to whether the Court decided correctly provides readers with a guide to making their own judgments on that score. Finally, editors' comments relating past and current Court cases to state and local issues helps readers evaluate the relevance of the Court to their concerns.

Ideology in Editorial Comment

Although people in the United States tend not to be ideological,[23] in relatively more obscure and arcane areas of politics and government ideological labels may guide citizens' understanding. Labels substitute for specific knowledge. "News reports," Johnson and Canon point out, "can be misleading. By their nature the media tend to simplify things."[24] Part of that simplification is the use of ideological shorthand, reporting events in right/left, conservative/liberal terms. Those terms provide a context from which the report derives some meaning, and reporters then hope that the meaning is clear to their readers.

In 1994, Justice Harry F. Blackmun announced his retirement and Stephen Breyer was nominated and confirmed for Blackmun's seat on the high court. This personnel change presented editors with the chance to write about the ideological balance on the bench and the position of the Justices on the ideological spectrum. Some editors took advantage of the opportunity.

The *Fresno Bee*, the *Jackson Clarion-Ledger*, and the *Providence Journal* all labeled Blackmun as "one of the Supreme Court's most stalwart liberals,"[25] or words to that effect. The *Bee* noted that, during his career on the Court, Blackmun moved "through . . . the spectrum of conventional political labels: moderate, conservative, liberal."[26] He ended up "the most liberal of the justices,"[27] which the *Bee* correctly attributes "to the court's dramatic shift to the right in the 1980s."[28] The picture is clear: Blackmun sides with the left on the court, and how the balance will shift depends on who his successor is.

Paper after paper described Clinton's nominee, Breyer, as a moderate. "He's a moderate, he's not an ideologue,"[29] the *Lincoln Journal* told its readers, as the *Albany Times-Union* made the same point: there was "no way of pinning an idealogue [*sic*] label to" the nominee.[30] The Albuquerque paper welcomed Breyer's nomination; it suggested that Clinton's choice of a moderate was influenced by the risk of a bruising confirmation battle had he named a strong liberal for the seat. The editors took the nomination as "a refreshing demonstration that high court nominees of moderate views and record" would fare better during confirmation and thereby keep "the Supreme Court from straying too far from the center."[31]

Perhaps surprisingly, editors rarely commented on the likely impact of the new nominee on the balance of left and right on the Court. Jackson readers were told that Breyer "will not upset the balance of the court,"[32] but they were not told what the balance of the Court was. Fresno editors labeled Breyer a "consensus builder," with the implication that he can work with both left and right on the Court but push the bench in neither direction.

The clearest statement about the impact of a new Justice on the ideological distribution on the Court came in passing. The *Lexington Herald-Leader* ran an editorial urging the Senate to examine Breyer's "sins" before voting on his nomination. The editors added, "The ideology of the Supreme Court can and does shift left or right, depending on who is in the White House when vacancies occur."[33] Exactly! But one searches in vain for an explanation of how Breyer's nomination fits.

Perhaps, had a conservative Justice retired, the editors would have seen Clinton's nominee as having a potentially greater effect on the Court's balance. But most editors did not even point out that Breyer's ascension to the bench would keep intact a relatively tenuous 5-to-4 split on several major sets of cases. The exception was the Jackson editor, who noted that "Clinton has the chance the [*sic*; the editor means "to"] preserve the current balance"[34] on the high court.

Editors did not, however, use ideological labels to describe either cases the Supreme Court has just decided or cases it was hearing for argument. Two editors wrote about the Arkansas term limits case[35] argued in late 1994. It presented a prime candidate for ideological discussion, given the sharp division between conservative Republicans who had been advocating term limits and more liberal Democrats opposed to the limits. Neither the Albany nor the Fresno editor wrote in ideological terms.[36] The editors, by the way, disagreed on the result the Court should reach.[37]

Editorials commenting on Court rulings were almost completely devoid of ideological references as well. The term saw a case challenging restrictions on protests at abortion clinics, use of preemptory challenges to exclude women from some juries, and conditions states may require before issuing permits to build. These cases present the kinds of issues on which one might expect disagreements along ideological lines. In fact, in the jury and gender case,[38] the *Albuquerque Journal* quoted both Justice Blackmun for the Court and Justice Antonin Scalia in dissent without characterizing the difference of opinion as ideological.[39]

Only two editorials used ideological labels in their commentary on Court decisions. The Court was unanimous in its ruling in *National Organization for Women v Scheidler*[40] that the federal Racketeer Influenced and Corrupt Organizations (RICO) Act can be applied to anti-abortion protests. Despite the fact that "all nine Justices—from Harry Blackmun and Ruth Bader Ginsburg on the liberal wing, to Antonin Scalia and Clarence Thomas on the right—join[ed] in a unanimous decision,"[41] the paper disagreed with the Court. The Raleigh editors described the 1993–1994 Court term as "marked by internal ideological division" and noted that the landuse case, *Dolan v. City of Tigard*[42] was decided "by a 5-4 conservative majority."[43]

Despite the guide to understanding high court dynamics that ideological shorthand could provide, editors generally shunned the use of the terms except when they were discussing individual members of the Court. The effect is that editors left their readers without these guides to assess the Justices and the Court's actions. Further, because the presence of these labels would have helped readers draw connections between the Court and the other branches where liberal and conservative terms are widely applied, editors subtly reinforce the notion that the Court is different from the more overtly political units of government.

The Court's Rulings

The Supreme Court takes few cases where all the good arguments fall on one side; clear-cut disputes of that nature do not call for clarification of the law or for the making of difficult choices. It follows, then, that the Court's rulings are likely to equally evoke disagreement as

agreement from observers and commentators. One might, indeed, expect more frequent disagreement than agreement from editors, if conflict with the Court's position makes for more dramatic and readable editorials.

When one examines local newspaper editorial responses to the Court's decisions, however, one finds much more agreement than disagreement. Seven editorials in four different newspapers took issue with a just-decided Supreme Court case. Twenty-five editorials from eight newspapers, however, agreed with the Court's decisions. *Fresno Bee* editors never objected to one of the rulings while it supported the outcomes nine times. *Albany Times-Union* editors thought the Court was wrong on two occasions, but five other times editors thought the Court reached the right result. Both the Raleigh and the Providence papers criticized two Court decisions; Raleigh editors agreed with the Court on two other occasions, but the Providence editors agreed only once.

Only on the case applying RICO to abortion protests did more editors (three) dissent from the Court's findings than concurred (two). Recall that the Court's decision was unanimous. But on abortion protest rules (four papers in support, none opposed), gender discrimination on juries (three versus one), and land-use restrictions (two versus one), a majority of the editors supported the Justices.

The language of the editorials supporting the Court's various decisions indicates the deference the editors accord the Court. One decision "carefully balances the rights of both sides";[44] another was "entirely consistent with a succession of rulings since 1987."[45] Yet another "should be applauded";[46] again, "the court got it right."[47]

Editors made few references to legal factors; their support tended to come from agreement with the policy implications of the outcome. Base closing decisions, for instance, "are too important to be left to the vagaries of politics and special interests," which is why the *Boise Idaho Statesman* supported the Court's ruling prohibiting challenges to the president's decision to close military installations.[48] Similarly, the *Raleigh News & Observer* supported the Court's decision on a "must-carry" regulation for local cable operators, calling it "a victory" for local television stations and "a triumph for consumers."[49]

Editorials taking exception to the Court's positions also focused on the policy effects. Lexington readers were urged to "[c]onsider the implications" of the Court's decision to apply the RICO Act to abortion protests. "[W]ith this ruling in place, the door is open for [RICO] to be used against any political movement—on the left or the right—that uses non-violent civil disobedience to make its point."[50] Raleigh readers were told that the Court's decision on the land-use case "just makes it harder for governments to protect one and all."[51]

A clear pattern emerges. From the perspective of these editorials, when the Supreme Court has spoken, it has probably taken the correct position. Editorial commentary on the Court's work, then, augments public support for the institution. At the very least, it provides no grist for the mill of discontent over the rulings from that tribunal.

Impact of the Court's Decisions

Although the Supreme Court's decisions bind the litigants involved, the impact of its pronouncements on others is not necessarily immediate or predictable. The larger impact of judicial policy as announced by the Court depends on how other affected populations respond. That response may be quite varied, because, as Johnson and Canon note, "many judicial decisions carry a great deal of latitude for interpretation and implementation."[52] In other words, for the Supreme Court to effect change through its decisions, a variety of other policymakers must make independent choices consistent with the Court's purpose. It is not the Supreme Court's rulings alone that matter: "Rather, rulings of the nation's highest court interact with those of other governmental agencies."[53]

Traditionally, scholars have examined compliance by taking a decision and seeing what consequences, if any, ensued after policymakers, opinion leaders, interest groups, and the general public responded to it. Actually, Supreme Court decisions may have a different effect on public life. They may establish the parameters within which acceptable policy may be made by state and local decisionmakers. The question is not so much whether policymakers adjust their behavior to correspond with guidelines the Court has handed down. Rather, it is whether they voluntarily take into account the strictures and expectations for their actions that may be deduced from the Supreme Court's opinions. Although it may occur years or decades after the Court decides a case, its impact is nevertheless significant. It is an impact that traditional studies of compliance with the Court's decisions would not find.

Editorial discussion of the relationship of past Court decisions to current state and local policy concerns emphasizes their relevance and makes the Court's rulings that much harder to ignore or avoid. Since politically active citizens are more likely to be readers of editorials than their more passive peers, editorial commentary on Court decisions helps frame the context within which decisionmakers view their alternatives.

These editorials show evidence of some of that kind of impact of the Court. Occasionally, editors cite a current decision that affects a policy decision being considered at the time. For instance, North Carolina had a tax on illegal drugs similar to one the Supreme Court ruled unconstitutional. When the state's Attorney General was "straining to distinguish" the North Carolina levy from the Montana one, the *Raleigh News & Observer* suggested that "North Carolina's tax [was] as flawed as Montana's."[54] Similarly, Jackson editors reminded legislators redrawing Mississippi's congressional districts, with creating black majority districts in mind, that "The U.S. Supreme Court ruled in June that such gerrymandering of districts to achieve a racial majority could not be extreme."[55]

Editorials bringing up past Court rulings, however, appeared more frequently. More than a dozen commentaries dealt with issues such as school prayer, illegal aliens, campaign spending limits, and groundwater use. When Nebraska faced the fact that petition circulators were being paid and considered whether that gave big money interests unfair advantages, the *Lincoln Journal* noted that an easy solution "would be to ban paid circulators. But the U.S. Supreme Court foreclosed that option in a 1988 ruling."[56] When a state legislator in Kentucky introduced a bill setting "absolute spending limits" on legislative campaigns, the *Lexington Herald-Leader* reminded everyone that "Such limits are plainly illegal. The Supreme Court has ruled that absolute limits violate constitutional guarantees of free speech."[57]

Occasionally, editors will assess how other states handle situations occurring at home, too. When the editors then bring in Supreme Court parameters, it is clearer that the initiative in introducing the Court's concerns into the local public discourse is theirs. Fresno editors thought that following Kansas City's example of devoting police resources to reduce carrying of illegal weapons would be worth emulating. The policy would be defensible, it said, because "[i]n recent years the U.S. Supreme Court has narrowed its definition of what is unreasonable"[58] in police searches. The Clinton administration, seeking to make public housing projects safer, proposed asking residents to sign permissions for random searches after a district court, applying Supreme Court precedents, had stopped warrantless searches in a Chicago housing project. The Albany paper rejected the idea, saying that "[a]s a practical matter . . . the new proposal may be every bit as reckless as that shot down by the Supreme Court."[59]

The number of instances here is not overwhelming, but even to this extent, editorials can and do serve to remind readers of relevant Supreme Court precedents that constrain policy options. Editorial commentary raises the salience of those precedents. "The salience of Supreme Court opinions," Kosaki and Franklin point out, is important "because of the implications it has for the possible impact of Court decisions."[60] If policymakers are aware of the limits on the alternatives the Court has set, they are potentially more likely to adhere to them.

CONCLUSION

The Supreme Court maintains high respect from editors around the nation. Its decisions receive positive evaluations, with only a minority of editorials criticizing the rulings the Court hands down. Editors also recognize the weight Supreme Court pronouncements carry by applying them on their own initiative to relevant local and state concerns. In these ways editors serve to underline the legitimacy of the Supreme Court as a governing institution in the nation.

Editors' limited use of ideological labels to identify voting coalitions on the Court and to characterize individual Justices serves to separate the Court from the other, more obviously political institutions of the national government. The Court and its members, being described differently and nonideologically, are set apart. Reporters who cover the Court, however, think of the Justices in more ideological terms. Davis reports that two out of three journalists "felt a justice's personal ideology is a very important factor in decision making."[61] If editors agree, they do a good job of hiding it from their readers.

The references in the editorials to the Supreme Court emphasized the interconnections between local concerns and national judicial outcomes. Such commentary has the effect of reducing the psychological distance between national decisionmakers and local residents. The deference the editors showed to the Court further suggests to readers that the Court deserves considerable respect. The role of the Court as a significant actor whose decisions the public should take seriously is thereby strengthened.

NOTES

1. Richard Funston, *A Vital National Seminar: The Supreme Court in American Political Life* (Palo Alto, Calif.: Mayfield, 1978), 218.

2. Funston, *A Vital National Seminar*, 217.

3. Jeffrey A. Segal and Harold J. Spaeth, *The Supreme Court and the Attitudinal Model* (Cambridge, Mass.: Cambridge University Press, 1993).

4. "High Court Criteria," *Albuquerque (New Mexico) Journal*, 11 April 1994, 6(A).

5. *Brown v. Board of Education*, 347 U.S. 483 (1954).

6. Gregory A. Caldeira, "Neither the Purse Nor the Sword: Dynamics of Public Confidence in the U.S. Supreme Court," *American Political Science Review* 80, no. 4 (December 1986): 1209.

7. Gregory A. Caldeira and James L. Gibson, "The Etiology of Public Support for the Supreme Court," *American Journal of Political Science* 36, no. 3 (August 1992): 636.

8. Caldeira and Gibson, "The Etiology of Public Support," 636.

9. Valerie J. Hoekstra, "The Supreme Court and Local Public Opinion," *American Political Science Review* 94, no. 1 (March 2000): 89–100.

10. Walter F. Murphy and C. Herman Pritchett, *Courts, Judges, and Politics: An Introduction to the Judicial Process*, 4th ed. (New York: Random House, 1986), 321.

11. Charles A. Johnson and Bradley C. Canon, *Judicial Policies: Implementation and Impact* (Washington, D.C.: Congressional Quarterly, 1984), 19.

12. David Ericson, "Newspaper Coverage of the Supreme Court: A Case Study," *Journalism Quarterly* 54, no. 3 (autumn 1977): 605–7; but see Stephanie Greco Larson, "How the New York *Times* Covered Discrimination Cases," *Journalism Quarterly* 62, no. 4 (winter 1985): 894–96.

13. Michael Solimine, "Newsmagazine Coverage of the Supreme Court," *Journalism Quarterly* 57, no. 4 (winter 1980): 661–63.

14. Elliot E. Slotnick and Jennifer A. Segal, "Television News and the Supreme Court" (paper presented at the annual meeting of the American Political Science Association, Chicago, Ill., September 1992).

15. Richard Davis, *The Press and American Politics: The New Mediator* (New York: Longman, 1992), 187.

16. Larry C. Berkson, *The Supreme Court and Its Publics* (Lexington, Mass.: Lexington Books, 1978).

17. David Paletz, *The Media in American Politics: Contents and Consequences* (New York: Longman, 1999), 296.

18. Melissa Gates and Jan P. Vermeer, "Reporting Supreme Court Decisions: Conflict, Dissents, and Other Cues" (paper presented at the annual meeting of the Western Political Science Association, San Francisco, Calif., March 1992).

19. Richard Davis, *Decisions and Images: The Supreme Court and the Press* (Englewood Cliffs, N.J.: Prentice-Hall, 1994), 21.

20. Lewis F. Powell Jr., "What Really Goes On at the Supreme Court," in *Judges on Judging: Views from the Bench*, ed. David M. O'Brien (Chatham, N.J.: Chatham House Publishers, 1997), 84.

21. Davis, *Decisions and Images*, 87.

22. Paletz, *The Media in American Politics*, 297.

23. M. Kent Jennings, "Ideological Thinking among Mass Publics and Political Elites," *Public Opinion Quarterly* 56, no. 4 (winter 1992): 419–41.

24. Johnson and Canon, *Judicial Policies*, 209.

25. "Blackmun's Legacy," *Providence (Rhode Island) Journal*, 7 April 1994, 8(A).

26. "Finding the Common Touch," *Fresno (California) Bee*, 8 April 1994, 8(B).

27. "Blackmun," *Jackson (Mississippi) Clarion-Ledger*, 7 April 1994, 12(A).

28. "Finding the Common Touch."

29. "Breyer: Opting for Brilliance," *Lincoln (Nebraska) Journal*, 17 May 1994, 8.

30. "Judge Breyer: A Good, Safe Choice," *Albany (New York) Times-Union*, 17 May 1994, 10(A).

31. "Breyer a Good Choice," *Albuquerque (New Mexico) Journal*, 17 May 1994, 6(A).

32. "Supreme Court: Stephen Breyer Should Be Confirmed," *Jackson (Mississippi) Clarion-Ledger*, 18 July 1994, 8(A).

33. "No Problem? Why Not?" *Lexington (Kentucky) Herald-Leader*, 16 July 1994, 14(A).

34. "Blackmun."

35. *U.S. Term Limits, Inc. v Thornton*, 514 U.S. 779 (1995).

36. "Term Limits, an Easy Choice," *Albany (New York) Times-Union*, 2 December 1994, 20(A); "The Constitution vs. Term Limits," *Fresno (California) Bee*, 27 November 1994, 6(B).

37. There was one other minor reference to ideology. In commenting on the Court's remand of a case dealing with free speech at CCNY for further consideration by a lower court, the Albany editors noted that "It would appear the high court, for all its conservative members, has climbed aboard the politically correct train." "Prof. Jeffries vs. CCNY," *Albany (New York) Times-Union*, 20 November 1994, 4(E).

38. *J.E.B. v. Alabama ex rel. T.B.*, 511 U.S. 127 (1994).

39. "Extending a Guarantee," *Albuquerque (New Mexico) Journal*, 22 April 1994, 14(A).

40. 510 U.S. 249 (1994).

41. "Uses of RICO," *Providence (Rhode Island) Journal*, 7 February 1994, 12(A).

42. 512 U.S. 374 (1994).

43. "Property Rights Extremes," *Raleigh (North Carolina) News & Observer*, 12 July 1994.

44. ". . . . And Welcome Rules on Protest," *Albany (New York) Times-Union*, 5 July 1994, 6(A).

45. "Proportionality and Land Use," *Fresno (California) Bee*, 4 July 1994, 6(B).

46. "Gender Ruling," *Jackson (Mississippi) Clarion-Ledger*, 22 April 1994.

47. "Free Speech: Clinic Ruling Favors Common Sense," *Lincoln (Nebraska) Journal*, 1 July 1994, 14.

48. "Keep Fairness in Base Closings," *Boise Idaho Statesman*, 25 May 1994, 13(A).

49. "Cable Ruling for Consumers," *Raleigh (North Carolina) News & Observer*, 2 July 1994.

50. "Is Dissent Racketeering?" *Lexington (Kentucky) Herald-Leader*, 26 January 1994, 8(A).

51. "Property Rights Extremes," *Raleigh (North Carolina) News & Observer*, 12 July 1994.

52. Johnson and Canon, *Judicial Policies*, 3.

53. David W. Neubauer, *Judicial Process: Law, Courts, and Politics in the United States* (Belmont, Calif.: Brooks/Cole Publishing Company, 1991), 416.

54. "Drug Tax Indefensible," *Raleigh (North Carolina) News & Observer*, 9 June 1994.

55. "Gerrymandering," *Jackson (Mississippi) Clarion-Ledger*, 2 January 1994, 4(C).

56. "Petitions: Giving Bonus to Citizen Action," *Lincoln (Nebraska) Journal*, 29 November 1994, 6.

57. "Worth a Try," *Lexington (Kentucky) Herald-Leader*, 4 February 1994, 14(A).

58. "Lessons from Kansas City," *Fresno (California) Bee*, 8 December 1994, 8(B).

59. "Don't Trample Tenant Rights," *Albany (New York) Times-Union*, 2 May 1994, 6(A).

60. Liane C. Kosaki and Charles H. Franklin, "Public Awareness of Supreme Court Decisions" (paper presented at the annual meeting of the Midwest Political Science Association, Chicago, Ill., April 1991), 3.

61. Davis, *Decisions and Images*, 146.

Chapter Seven

Protecting the States

If there exists a more complicated system of government in the world than the federalism used in the United States, few people know of it. Citizens have to deal with a formidable array of governments—national, state, county, frequently a city government, and almost always several special districts with responsibility for specific tasks. If these units of government all had their own spheres of authority, perhaps the public could learn to understand the system better, but federalism in the United States entails a complex sharing of functions and overlapping authority. Who, for instance, is responsible for an error in highway construction, the national government that provided most of the funds, the state that chose the route and specified the process for selecting a contractor, or the county that oversaw the construction?

"Such complications," Glendening and Reeves say, "are the price Americans pay for the diversity within the governmental system."[1] It is a price that presents editors with an unending stream of political problems crying out for attention. Should the national government act? California's governor Pete Wilson "has again reached out his hand to Congress to cover the costs of providing services to illegal immigrants,"[2] reports the *Fresno Bee*. Should the national government not act or stop taking action? The *Boise Idaho Statesman* hoped the people of their state would elect "a strong chief executive who will stand up to the federal government over the issue of nuclear waste."[3]

MAKING FEDERALISM WORK

States find themselves in the precarious situation of facing problems that transcend their boundaries without sufficient resources, whether fiscal or political, to respond adequately. When drivers in California stop buying automobiles made in Detroit, for example, Michigan's unemployment goes up at the same time the state's revenues derived from income and sales taxes decline. Yet the internal political pressures to act are strong. Voters demand results, and governors and other state leaders want to point to successful accomplishments for future political campaigns.

Federal systems, at a minimum, distribute power among levels of government while protecting the continuing existence of each level. Elezar's definition ("Federalism can be defined as the mode of political organization that unites separate polities within an overarching political system by distributing power among general and constituent governments in a manner designed to protect the existence and authority of both")[4] highlights both the authority to act and the separate existence of each level. But independent existence and authority to act do not suffice if the problems overwhelm the resources.

As a consequence, over the course of American history, federalism has evolved into a cooperative arrangement between the national government and the states. It combines a great deal of "policy centralization" with "continued reliance on subnational governmental implementation" of those policies.[5] Welfare, education, health care, agriculture, transportation, energy—the list of areas where primacy in setting the policy lies with Washington but where state agencies typically administer most of the programs is seemingly endless. Only with consultation and cooperation does the system work.

The inevitable disagreements cannot be readily resolved. Technically, through the Constitution's Supremacy Clause, the national government's positions prevail against opposing state concerns. However, the Supremacy Clause formally comes into play only when the dispute between state and national governments goes to court. At any other time, negotiations and bargaining characterize the process through which discord is handled. The threat to invoke the Supremacy Clause, of course, carries great weight, but in the meantime, accommodation presents a preferred outcome.

Were ways of resolving disagreements as simple as just suggested, however, less animosity would mark national and state relationships.

However, the national government essentially negotiates with all states at the same time; that is, it develops and administers a policy in conjunction with all fifty states. When a consensus emerges on a program, one or more states may feel their interests ignored. But accommodating those states undermines that agreement. National flexibility does not extend that far. To make policy work, then, "[f]ederal officials seek cooperative compliance on the part of the states," notes Elezar, "knowing that such compliance is more effective in the long run."[6] States may not always be willing to comply.

National policy and state programs intertwine considerably, then. Although it is not possible to say what proportion of state policies are linked to national policies, clearly significant segments of state action mesh—or clash—with national activity. These connections present the clearest instances of the relevance of national political institutions to local citizens. Who pays for highways, who decides school curriculum questions, who controls the purity of drinking water, and who checks to see if the workplace is safe matter to virtually everyone. State governments and their local governments work with, and sometimes against, the national government in these matters.

How states protect their interests poses interesting questions. Elezar posits two methods. One builds on the states' representation in Congress and the use those representatives make of legislative oversight and casework on behalf of the state. The second relies on the ongoing relationship between state agencies and their national counterparts.[7] One might think a third would be to arouse public opinion in support of the state.[8]

National–state relationships provide editors with a great deal of material for commentary. Whether their words strike a responsive chord among citizens we cannot say; when they bother, however, to make the effort, attentive readers cannot help but be reminded of the extent to which national programs affect their own concerns. Perhaps a local project receives a boost from federal help, such as an "AmeriCorps crew . . . helping state farmers in six watersheds protect their groundwater supplies."[9] Perhaps it is federal action that pre-empts state regulation of what editors consider a local matter: "[W]hat is the justification for federal intervention in local and state regulation of businesses operating almost exclusively within a state's borders?"[10] Either way, editors have a lot to say to their readers about how federalism works for them in practice.

EDITORIAL COMMENTARY

Editors' concern with policy outcomes motivates their editorial commentary. Abstract notions of federalism, constitutional authority, and formal divisions of power matter not as much as what happens in protecting water quality, funding roads and other state projects, and regulating agriculture appropriately. Editors therefore wind up adopting two positions on federalism: one asks the national government to act decisively, and the other asks the national government to step aside and let states handle matters for themselves. In each case, a desire to reach preferred policy results outweighs constitutional niceties.

National Action Welcomed

Sometimes a state simply cannot act successfully without help. When Mississippi considered various ways to ensuring that parents made court-ordered child support payments, Jackson editors welcomed a federal proposal "to improve collections from deadbeat dads."[11] After an AMTRAK derailment in North Carolina, *News & Observer* editors thought "a study . . . of rail safety issues is necessary and timely."[12] Similarly, new Food and Drug Administration labeling requirements for dietary supplements, the *Fresno Bee* said, "are reasonable," while they do not prevent "anyone from buying rhino horn and garlic pills in the hope of putting hair on his chest and zest in his love life."[13]

When states and localities lack either resources or authority—or both—to deal effectively with conditions that confront them, federal action may be the only reasonable alternative available. In these instances, editors see the national government as acting responsibly and in the public interest. Frequently enough, the national government must be spurred to action, and editors are more than willing to provide the impetus with appropriately worded commentary.

The *Lincoln Journal* strongly supported the Clinton administration's proposal to raise the cost of a license to sell guns, in large part to reduce the number in its area. "In Lancaster County [Lincoln's county] alone there were 345 federally licensed firearms dealers. . . . There are only eight McDonald's restaurants."[14] When the U.S. Senate moved to weaken drinking water purity standards, the *Albany Times-Union* protested, urging legislators to keep the standards high. "[B]acking down from the goal of pure water is the wrong way to go." National action upholding high standards is needed because "local governments . . . are hard-pressed for revenue" and will not meet the standards on their own. They need "financial assistance . . . to help them comply" with the standards, so "the public health shouldn't be compromised."[15]

Asking for federal money to attain local goals occurs relatively frequently, too. Don't make "any changes that would reduce federal commitment" to the Women, Infants and Children program in Mississippi, the Jackson editors urged. "There are a lot of programs that don't work, but WIC is not one of them. WIC works for Mississippi's babies."[16] When the federal government denied a grant application to keep a shelter for homeless teenagers (Crossroads) operating, the *Lansing State Journal* published several editorials to encourage citizens to "start by complaining to their representatives in Congress. Crossroads is the kind of 'pork' that some congressmen complained about during the recent crime bill debate. . . . If Crossroads is pork, we say, serve up another helping."[17]

National Action Opposed

More often editors preferred that the national government refrain from taking a role. The *Boise Idaho Statesman* editors, concerned about possible federal decisions on protecting parts of the state as wilderness, made the general point that underlies most editors' objections to federal action: "Idahoans are best qualified to determine the future of the backcountry."[18]

The clash of interests and perspectives between the state's citizens and the national government lies at the heart of editors' concern with national action. The national government does not understand local conditions: Because "communities that draw water from a surface source" have different contamination problems than "cities that get their water from below ground," the *Lincoln Journal* argued, "[s]tates need to have a role in . . . guiding action."[19] Nor does the national government have the same priorities. In arguing that the California Public Utilities Commission should set rates in a new natural gas pipeline rather than the Federal Energy Regulatory Commission, the *Fresno Bee* argued that "the PUC has a duty that the feds do not to set rates in a way that balances costs and benefits, protects residential customers, maintains service for low-income families and promotes such desirable social goals as energy conservation and the development of alternative fuel vehicles."[20]

Sometimes federal actions simply make no sense to editors. "Congress . . . should leave regulation of the tow-truck industry to state and local regulators," the *Albuquerque Journal* said. "[W]hat is the justification for federal intervention in local and state regulation of businesses operating almost exclusively within a state's borders?"[21] Calling it "[o]ne of the dumber Bush era war-on-drugs laws," the *Bee* thought California ought to object to the requirement that they "suspend the driver's licenses of all convicted drug criminals." Besides legal considerations, the paper disliked the "likely effect." It would "increase the number of people driving without a license and therefore without insurance. To what benefit?"[22]

Federal action coordinated with state and local officials received a somewhat better reception, as long as the state interests are protected. The *Bee* welcomed a "new agreement between state and federal water agencies" because environmental needs were balanced with the needs of "urban and agricultural water users."[23] The *Jackson Clarion-Ledger* praised the cooperation between the U.S. Department of Justice and local officials in improving conditions in jails where the suicide rate had been "disturbing." It contrasted the cooperation with "confrontational orders and resistance"[24] that otherwise might have been the expected.

Perceptions of Federalism

It is hard to imagine a governmental system more tied to juridical foundations than federalism. U.S. federalism was developed as much by courts as it was by the Constitution and by the actions of Congress and the president. Yet editors approach questions of federalism, with minor exceptions, from a very different standpoint. To them, federalism is a political fact of life that frequently causes problems but that one must live with and adapt to. From the perspective of the editors of these daily newspapers, the federalism they espouse might be called pragmatic federalism.

Glendening and Reeves clearly describe what editors have in mind: "By pragmatic federalism we mean a constantly adjusting arrangement fashioned to current needs with an emphasis on problem-solving and a minimal adherence to rigid doctrine."[25] Theories of federalism serve academics, but they do not help editors. Editors' concerns center on effective responses to the problems facing the public, and if the federal arrangement can be used to fix those problems, it should be used; otherwise, policymakers should bypass it.

Time and again editors call upon local representatives in Congress to uphold the state's interests while Washington makes policy. Boise editors pointed with pride to an Idaho senator and a representative working together to protect birds of prey. It was, they said, "proof that Idaho's congressional delegation can get something done when it pulls together."[26] Similarly, the Albuquerque paper praised their members for getting a clause in an appropriations bill that would keep a lunchroom open at Carlsbad Caverns. "Fortunately," it noted, the New Mexico delegation "worked to put the brakes on the Park Service recommendation" to close the eatery. The effort to close the lunchroom was "an elitist, unnecessary move imposed by a vast federal bureaucracy on a harmless business."[27]

When nothing else can be done, the editors usually recommend simply buckling down and complying with federal regulations. *Bee* editors reluctantly agree with Fresno State's settling a Title IX case out of court, leading to the elimination of the men's swimming team. "The fact is that Title IX is the law, and if its detractors wish to fight it, the battlefield is the halls of Congress."[28] Lincoln editors disapproved of the state's governor and its attorney general's opposing a federal requirement that Medicaid cover abortions resulting from rape or incest. The governor, Ben Nelson, "vowed . . . to fight it. But the law," the paper said, "is on the side of Congress and the federal government," urging Nelson to "abandon a futile legal effort."[29]

The area of federalism that caused some editors the most consternation dealt with "unfunded mandates." The *Idaho Statesman* was particularly concerned, running six editorials on the subject itself. "Federal laws," it explained, "on such things as clean water, drug use, labor relations and air quality require local taxpayers to foot the bill if Congress chooses, as it often does, not to send along a check for expenses."[30] These mandates, the editors explained, put local governments in an awkward situation. "To get the needed funds, cities and counties will have to take it from local priorities. . . . Or they will have to raise taxes."[31] Providence readers learned why Congress likes an unfunded mandate so well: It "allows legislators in Washington to take credit for promoting ambitious measures having to pay the costs out of the federal budget."[32]

Not all the editors were as negative about mandates as these examples suggested. The Jackson editors thought the mandates could be made to work if they "at least consider and lay out projected costs to local communities," suggesting "transition funds" along the way.[33] *Lincoln Journal* editors reminded their readers that "even unfunded federal mandates address desirable goals and that there have to be mandates from somewhere—federal, state, or local—to set standards and cover reasonable costs associated with such problems as prison overcrowding, water pollution and poor people without health insurance."[34]

It was clear, however, that the overwhelming perception among editors was that unfunded mandates represented a real problem in federalism. Not only do they separate the responsibility for funding from the credit for the program, they force states and localities to choose between desired services and higher taxes. Therefore, when welfare reform proposals began to include moving programs to the states, the *Fresno Bee* cautioned policymakers: "Washington must also fund the transfer adequately. Giving the states freedom to reform welfare without enough money to do the job right would be a step backward."[35]

Unfunded mandates presented an unfortunate fact of political life. In accordance with pragmatic federalism, however, editors who saw these mandates as a problem looked for political options. Change in congressional legislation, for instance, was one such option. Not only did the Boise paper applaud local representative Dirk Kempthorne's bill to end unfunded mandates, they also welcomed a Senate vote to "ease regulations in the Safe Drinking Water Act," a law the paper called "so Draconian that no one has been able to meet all its dictates."[36]

The Tobacco Issue

Few subjects are as local in nature as agriculture. Since the New Deal, the national government has, of course, been deeply involved in agricultural policies of various sorts, from price supports to acreage limitations. States and localities, however, continue to play a vital role in agriculture, tied up as it is in the economies of small and large communities throughout rural America. In two states tobacco has been a major cash crop, supporting generations of farmers. But since the rise of the antismoking concerns in recent decades, the future of tobacco farming has been cast in doubt.

Accordingly, both the *Raleigh News & Observer* and the *Lexington Herald-Leader* editors paid close attention to movement in Washington on tobacco issues. The major proposal in 1994 was to raise cigarette taxes by up to $1.25 a pack and to use part of the proceeds to redevelop tobacco-growing areas. At stake was the future of tobacco farming, already under siege because of imports of cheaper tobacco. The tide of public opinion was flowing strongly against smoking, but the burden of antitobacco legislation was going to be felt most strongly by the local growers of tobacco in Kentucky and North Carolina.

The *News & Observer*, while sympathetic to the farmers' plight, urged the state's representatives in Congress to be realistic. "They would help their constituents much more by supporting a sizable increase" in the cigarette tax, instead of opposing it automatically, "on the condition that a good portion of it benefits North Carolina farmers."[37] The Lexington editors took a similar tack: local representatives are mistaken when they say, "Defeat the tax . . . and save tobacco." Instead, they should accept reality. "The same law that levies a new tax on tobacco also should set aside money for the redevelopment of tobacco-growing counties."[38]

The *Lexington Herald-Leader* was especially strident in its urging of support for a higher cigarette tax coupled with money for redevelopment. Editors minced no words. Politicians who opposed the idea demonstrated a "bullheaded resistance to the facts of life."[39] Editors were frustrated with "Kentucky's congressmen [who] refuse to discuss the idea that the cigarette tax could be a sheep in wolf's clothing."[40] By turning their backs on the possibility of up to $337 million dollars in relief funds,[41] "farm leaders have ignored a sensible way for rural communities to survive. It is a shame and a trust broken."[42] The paper had kind words only for Governor Brereton Jones who took the same position the editors did. "For his trouble, the governor has been chastened like a chicken-killing dog."[43]

Both the Raleigh and the Lexington papers were then caught somewhat off guard when North Carolina Representative Charles Rose proposed ending the allotment system (tobacco's price support system) and financing the allotment buy-out by a cigarette tax increase. Both papers were skeptical of Rose's motives. Attributing the point of view to "tobacco insiders," Lexington editors raised the possibility that "Ol' Charley . . . is just yanking the cigarette companies' chains. He wants the companies to buy more American tobacco."[44] The *News & Observer* voiced similar suspicions. If the tobacco companies "agreed to take" surplus tobacco now held by a farmer-financed co-op, "Rose presumably would shelve his proposal."[45]

Both papers, however, gave Rose the benefit of the doubt. Raleigh editors said the proposal "could be good public policy and smart economics. . . . [I]t warrants a serious look."[46] In Lexington, readers were told that "a buy-out program makes sense, particularly if combined with a tobacco-state redevelopment fund. Charlie Rose, one of tobacco's own, is thinking that way."[47] In the minds of the editors, Rose's idea could achieve some national objectives consistent with the goals of anti-smoking forces while protecting local interests. That is an ideal combination for generating editorial support.

Other Local Concerns with National Policy

The three most western newspapers in this study, from New Mexico, Idaho, and California, took disparate positions on proposals from the Clinton administration to raise grazing fees on public lands and to impose stricter rangeland reforms. The issue is one at the heart of federalism: how much local control is consistent with the achievement of national objectives? How much deference should national policymakers give to local interests?

The *Albuquerque Journal* took the strongest stand in favor of local interests. "Local residents . . . can provide perspectives that would be missing from edicts handed down by Washington."[48] The editors were particularly concerned about the survival of the small ranchers. "Humans are part of the ecosystem, too. The needs of the people who have lived here for generations deserve to be weighed against the ecological theories of those who came here much later."[49] The paper raised concerns about the decision process, hoping to ensure that all relevant perspectives be taken into account. "Important decisions on the use of America's public lands should be made by the public."[50]

Neither the Boise nor the Fresno editors were as concerned with local interests. For the *Idaho Statesman*, it was a question of finances. Congress, it said, should focus "on what is best for taxpayers, as well as all users of the land." It supported a balance between a "policy that will neither cripple the ranching industry nor allow public land to be abused. And it cannot do harm to the nation's finances."[51] The *Bee*'s concern supported "the setting of national environmental standards designed to curtail the trampling and overgrazing of range and watersheds."[52] Fresno readers were warned against a proposal to create advisory councils that "could well be dominated by local politics and economic interests."[53] The Idaho and California editors, then, were much more receptive toward national concerns than the New Mexico editors.

Typically when one thinks of local concerns in a federal context, NIMBY (Not In My Back Yard) issues come to mind. Surprisingly, very few editorials took that stance. Disposal of nuclear waste, unsurprisingly, provided the impetus for three editorials, one from New Mexico and two from Idaho, raising a NIMBY objection. The Mescalero Apache people offered to lease utilities temporary storage space for spent nuclear rods. The Albuquerque editors did not oppose the project outright, but it did suggest that the "project should be delayed" until safety concerns are fully resolved. "The backyard may be huge and mostly empty, but it is *all of our* backyard."[54] The *Boise Idaho Statesman* applauded incoming Governor Phil Batt's stand against shipments of more nuclear waste to an ostensibly temporary storage site in Idaho. Although the editors recognize that "a long term solution . . . belongs in Washington," they add "Batt cannot let Idaho become a de facto nuclear waste dump for the nation."[55]

CONCLUSION

Connections between policy decisions reached in Washington and those being debated in states and localities form the fabric of federalism in the United States. Especially in areas where both national and state levels of government exercise legitimate authority, sound public policy calls for consultation, accommodation, and cooperation between officials at the two levels. Daily newspaper editors clearly support this kind of interaction among federal and state policymakers. For them, it is how government ought to operate.

If federalism is going to operate reasonably well, each level must be aware of and recognize the relevance of the other levels of the system. Just as national decisionmakers must take into account the variety of circumstances across the nation where their policies will have to be applied, state and local leaders cannot ignore national priorities that overlap with their concerns. Editorials helped ensure that state and local elites take national perspectives into account in their deliberations.

Editors approach federalism questions quite pragmatically. Rarely is it a question of who has authority to act; it is most often a question of who will take the right action. Policy outcomes, not legal niceties, dominate editorial commentary. For instance, although editors repeatedly recognized that Washington's decisions would ultimately prevail over local preferences, given a conflict between the two, not one editor over the course of the entire year mentioned the Supremacy Clause or the "necessary and proper" clause as the basis for national authority.

Editors subordinate theoretical federalism questions, such as the contrast between the "compact" and the "national" theories of federalism Cantril and Cantril discuss,[56] to preferred outcomes.

For the most part, editors were protective of local interests. When they wanted the national government to act, editors usually had a local concern or policy outcome in mind. When they wanted the national government to stay out, they again usually wanted to guard localities and their concerns. Time and again they called on local members in Congress to step in, and they applauded them when they did so successfully.

Editors' pragmatic federalism coincides with a somewhat troubling conception—editors seem to think that federal policy should be infinitely adjustable to reflect local conditions. They are aware of the need for consistency from place to place, for uniformity as a means of treating every one fairly. They are nevertheless convinced that the diversity on which the federal system is built calls for a discretionary adjustment to take the special circumstances of the editors' home state into account. In other words, editors are willing to sacrifice the values of consistency and uniformity on the altar of diversity if it means the adoption of workable policies for their areas.

Ultimately, the extensive editorial commentary reviewed here emphasizes once again the extent to which editors consider decisions reached in Washington relevant to their readers. By highlighting federal issues and by commenting on their connections to local concerns, these editors help to ensure that state policymakers take Washington developments into account. The prime example is the effort of the *Lexington Herald-Leader* editors to keep the option of a high cigarette tax coupled with money for economic redevelopment in the forefront of officials' thinking, despite the fact that only the state's governor seemed to share that position. Editors' discussions of federal issues, then, stimulate state and local policymakers to look outwardly, toward the nation's capital as well as inwardly, to the area's problems and concerns. That constitutes a worthwhile contribution to public discourse.

NOTES

1. Parris N. Glendening and Mavis Mann Reeves, *Pragmatic Federalism: An Intergovernmental View of American Government* (Pacific Palisades, Calif.: Palisades Publishers, 1977), 2.
2. "Budgeting by Prayer," *Fresno (California) Bee*, 10 January 1994, 6(B).

3. "Batt Will Need to Stand Firm Against Nuke Waste Storage," *Boise Idaho Statesman*, 11 December 1994.

4. Daniel J. Elezar, *American Federalism: A View from the States*, 2nd ed. (New York: Thomas Y. Crowell Company, 1972), 2.

5. David B. Walker, *The Rebirth of Federalism: Slouching toward Washington* (Chatham, N.J.: Chatham House Publishing, 1995), 3.

6. Elezar, *American Federalism*, 162.

7. Elezar, *American Federalism*, 158–63.

8. One is reminded of Justice Felix Frankfurter's dissent in *Baker v Carr*, 369 U.S. 186 (1962): "Appeal must be to an informed, civically militant electorate. . . . In a democratic society like ours, relief must come through an aroused popular conscience that sears the conscience of the people's representatives."

9. "AmeriCorps: Grand Push for the River," *Lansing (Michigan) State Journal*, 6 October 1994, 8(A).

10. "Congress Shouldn't Stop State Tow Truck Rules," *Albuquerque (New Mexico) Journal*, December 5, 1994, 8(A).

11. "Child Support: Tough Federal/State Efforts Needed," *Jackson (Mississippi) Clarion-Ledger*, 1 July 1994, 14(A).

12. Signals Up for Rail Safety," *Raleigh (North Carolina) News & Observer*, 20 May 1994.

13. "Rhino Horn and Crocodile Fears," *Fresno (California) Bee*, 4 January 1994, 4(B).

14. "Guns: U.S. Doesn't Need a Dealer on Every Block," *Lincoln (Nebraska) Journal*, 10 January 1994, 6.

15. " . . . And Don't Weaken Standards," *Albany (New York) Times-Union*, 31 May 1994, 10(A).

16. "WIC: Mississippi Needs This Vital Program," *Jackson (Mississippi) Clarion-Ledger*, 25 November 1994, 14(A).

17. "Crossroads: We Cannot Stand Idly By and Let Teen Shelter Close," *Lansing (Michigan) State Journal*, 9 October 1994, 8(A).

18. "California Makes Progress," *Boise Idaho Statesman*, April 15, 1994.

19. "Safe Water: It Belongs with Essential Services," *Lincoln (Nebraska) Journal*, 13 March 1994, 2(B).

20. "Fair Play for Mojave," *Fresno (California) Bee*, 14 January 1994, 4(B).

21. "Congress Shouldn't Stop State Tow-Truck Rules," *Albuquerque (New Mexico) Journal*, 5 December 1994, 8(A)8.

22. "Dumb Drug Laws," *Fresno (California) Bee*, 19 April 1994, 6(B).

23. "A Truce in the Delta," *Fresno (California) Bee*, 23 December 1994, 6(B).

24. "Jails: Justice/Local Agreements Positive," *Jackson (Mississippi) Clarion-Ledger*, 21 September 1994, 10(A).

25. Glendening and Reeves, *Pragmatic Federalism*, 8.

26. "Idaho's U.S. Delegation Can Pull Together for Good of State," *Boise Idaho Statesman*, 24 May 1994.

27. "New Mexico's Congressmen Rescue Caverns' Eatery," *Albuquerque (New Mexico) Journal*, 28 July 1994, 18(A).

28. "Toward Gender Equity," *Fresno (California) Bee*, 14 March 1994, 4(B).

29. "Medicaid: Skip the Lawyering," *Lincoln (Nebraska) Journal*, 7 September 1994, 16.

30. "Cities Need Relief from Mandates," *Boise Idaho Statesman*, 24 January 1994.

31. "Federal Mandates Strain Local Government Budgets," *Boise Idaho Statesman*, 23 May 1994, 5(A).

32. "Those Mobile Mandates," *Providence (Rhode Island) Journal*, 4 December 1994, 14(B).

33. "Mandates: Somebody Has to Pay the Bills," *Jackson (Mississippi) Clarion-Ledger*, 30 July 1994, 10(A).

34. "New Federalism: Beware of Quick Fixes," *Lincoln (Nebraska) Journal*, 29 December 1994, 16.

35. "Welfare Federalism," *Fresno (California) Bee*, 25 November 1994, 8(B).

36. "Federal Mandates."

37. "A Tax for the Farmer," *Raleigh (North Carolina) News & Observer*, February 13, 1994.

38. "Face Reality on Tobacco," *Lexington (Kentucky) Herald-Leader*, 15 May 1994, 1(E).

39. "Bullheaded and Blindfolded," *Lexington (Kentucky) Herald-Leader*, 31 July 1994, 1(E).

40. "A New Response to Cigarette Taxes," *Lexington (Kentucky) Herald-Leader*, 10 July 1994, 1(E).

41. "A $1 Billion Loss for Farmers," *Lexington (Kentucky) Herald-Leader*, 3 July 1994, 1(E).

42. "Enjoy the 'Victory' While It Lasts," *Lexington (Kentucky) Herald-Leader*, 25 September 1994, 1(F).

43. "A Lone Voice of Sense on Tobacco," *Lexington (Kentucky) Herald-Leader*, 28 August 1994, 1(H).

44. "U-Turn on Tobacco Road," *Lexington (Kentucky) Herald-Leader*, 1 October 1994, 14(A).

45. "Rose's Surprising Plan," *Raleigh (North Carolina) News & Observer*, 2 October 1994.

46. "Rose's Surprising Plan."

47. "U-Turn on Tobacco Road."

48. "Tall in the Saddle." *Albuquerque (New Mexico) Journal*, 16 January 1994, 2(B).

49. "Hear All the Voices." *Albuquerque (New Mexico) Journal*, 23 January 1994, 2(B).

50. "Overseeing Public Lands." *Albuquerque (New Mexico) Journal*, 16 February 1994, 10(A).

51. "Congress Can Fix Grazing Issue with Focus on Budget," *Boise Idaho Statesman*, 23 December 1994.

52. "Home, Home on the Dole," *Fresno (California) Bee*, 31 December 1994, 4(B).

53. "Toward Grazing Reform?" *Fresno (California) Bee*, 13 March 1994, 10(B).

54. "Lots of Empty Backyard." *Albuquerque (New Mexico) Journal*, 13 March 1994, 2(B) (italics in original).

55. "Batt Will Need to Stand Firm."

56. Albert H. Cantril and Susan Davis Cantril, *Reading Mixed Signals: Ambivalence in American Public Opinion about Government* (Washington, D.C.: Woodrow Wilson Center Press, 1999), 37.

Chapter Eight

Through the Prism
of Local Priorities

When national politics intrudes upon local lives, editors of daily newspapers have no qualms about going on the offensive. Editors are even more likely to defend local interests when basic values can be invoked ("It is and always has been fundamental to the health of a democracy that the government not lie to, manipulate or directly harm the very people who have given it life.").[1] When the occasion is the release of federal government documents detailing radiation experiments on retarded youngsters conducted more than forty years ago in Massachusetts, the temptation to attack is virtually irresistible; after all, who would justify those experiments now? And so the *Providence Journal* bravely took the Department of Energy to task, championing openness in government and decrying the "national Pandora's box" that the report opened.[2]

As we have seen, most editorial commentary on national politics takes a more realistic and fitting approach. Editors used their columns in 1994 as a way to discuss with their readers perspectives and positions that would be out of place in the news columns. Here editors weighed in on the significant issues of the day, and the fact that so often editors found those issues to deal with politics and political institutions in Washington testifies to the significance the editors placed on national political matters.

PUTTING IT ALL TOGETHER

The plain finding in this study is that local newspaper editorials comment frequently on national political affairs and institutions. That commentary carries the strong likelihood that the ideas broached there enter local public discourse. Among frequent readers of editorials, the fact of repeated editorials devoted to national politics reinforces the relevance of national concerns. The underlying themes implicit in the editorials can, by their repetition, affect the way local publics view what happens in Washington and in the nation.

The ten newspapers in this study varied considerably in the extent to which the editors introduced national political considerations into local political discourse. From the *Fresno Bee*'s extensive editorializing on everything having to do with politics in the nation's capital and beyond, to the *Lansing State Journal*'s virtual ignoring of anything that happened outside Michigan, editors exercised considerable discretion in their selection of topics for their editorials. Clearly, but not exclusively, they were motivated by the big stories of the year for their subjects. The more important the national news story, the more likely that local newspapers would carry an editorial on it. Although editors were audience-driven to a large degree, they were also news-driven in their choice of editorial topics.

Congress and its members frequently benefited—and also suffered—from extensive editorial criticism. Local members, as expected, got laurels rather than brickbats, and members from other areas bore the brunt of editorial criticism. So did the institution itself. Editors saw Congress as cumbersome, consumed with personal and special interests, and blind to the public interest, as the editors identified it. But underneath their criticism lay the notion that Congress as a whole deserved respect. The problems, editors thought, resulted from other members misusing the body. Were procedures to be reformed so that misguided legislators from other parts of the country could not abuse the legislative process, Congress would operate well in the service of the nation as it was intended. And so editors subtly reinforced support for the institution as it criticized its operation.

President Clinton did not enjoy a good year in 1994; editorial commentary did not spare him. Nevertheless, editors gave him center stage compared to Congress. The nation's international and domestic direction depended on his choices. Editors believed his primacy over Congress relegated the legislature to the role of something equivalent to that of a staff aide: checking for mistakes and carrying out presidential tasks. Editors spent so much time and attention on the president that readers could not be faulted for thinking of the president and the national government as being virtually one and the same.

It is not, of course. No president can keep track of and control everything the federal bureaucracy, for instance, does. But what the bureaucracy does, editors do not particularly like. This pattern parallels Hibbing and Theiss-Morse's conclusion about the public and policy: "People are much less pleased," they find, "with the government's processes than its polices [*sic*]."[3] Editors' criticisms of federal agencies reinforce long-standing stereotypes about bureaucracies, especially disregard for local needs and being out of touch with the real world people live in. Editors were quick to charge that agency decisions ran counter to basic American values, but they relaxed their standards when outcomes they agreed with were involved. Overall, editors did little to strengthen citizens' respect for the federal bureaucracy, but their extensive commentary served the purpose of emphasizing the prominence of these agencies in people's everyday lives.

Less prominent in national news, the Supreme Court was also much less visible in these editorials. Neither individual justices, save for the retiring Justice Blackmun and the newly appointed Justice Breyer, nor voting blocs on the bench generated much editorial comment. Significantly, however, when editors commented on decisions the Court handed down, they most often thought the Court was correct. Although they criticized some decisions, most notably one that permitted the use of the RICO Act against abortion protesters, they gave readers the impression that the Court generally reaches the appropriate result. By avoiding ideological labels and discussions of voting alliances and splits on the Court, the editors unconsciously reinforced the notion that the Court stands apart from, and even above, politics as usual. By occasionally bringing in past Court decisions in discussions of current state and local issues, editors also extend the impact of court rulings. These considerations enter into public discourse and help shape the constraints within which state and local policy will be made.

Editors demonstrated more concern with state and local interests, quite appropriately so, given their markets, than with national concerns. When the two intersected, editors championed state perspectives. Even when they realized that the Constitution grants supremacy to national government actions over state policies, editors argued for taking local voices into account. The pragmatic federalism they advocated was a federalism that gave leeway to state and local governments and provided the national government with enough latitude to adjust its programs to account for local conditions. The national government, therefore, could be helpful, and if it were not, editors argued for giving state prerogatives a broader scope.

A PARADOXICAL VIEW FROM THE STATES

The overall impression that emerges from this review of local daily newspaper editorials is a contradictory sense of separation and connection between national politics on the one hand and state and local concerns on the other. The separation arises out of the frequent contrasts editors draw between what makes good policy for the state versus what national leaders propose. The connection comes out of the sheer number of times editors choose to highlight a national development in an editorial, thereby "signalizing"[4] the importance of those events for their state and local readers. National political institutions and processes cannot be ignored, editors told their readers, because they affect what we here at home can and cannot accomplish.

The contrast with the national media is great. Editorials in the national media begin with the assumption that political developments in Washington are relevant to their readers. National editors have no reason to draw connections between national and local affairs as a general rule. They rarely find it necessary to argue that an otherwise useful national policy should be changed because of detrimental effects in one or two localities. Editors in the national media can approach national politics without having to justify their attention in state or local terms.

By regularly bringing forward issues emerging out of national politics and by commenting frequently, whether positively or negatively, on national political institutions, local editors inject these matters into local public discourse. Highlighting in an editorial a mistaken judgment a federal bureaucrat may have made raises readers' awareness of the problem; praising a policy proposal as one likely to be acceptable to national leaders increases the probability that local decisionmakers will take it seriously. By their comments on national politics, editors make it harder for others to ignore national developments and policies.

Further, it may very well take drawing a local connection to make national politics relevant to the paper's readers. Mondak found, for instance, that "coattail voting occurs when the voter can *meaningfully connect* national and subnational campaigns."[5] The important concept here is in the italicized phrase. Mondak goes on to suggest that "[t]he political world . . . may seem distant and highly abstract if the citizen is denied local perspective."[6] He concludes with recommendations for newspapers: "when reporting on national political events, newspapers should emphasize the story's local significance."[7] That is exactly what the editors of these newspapers did in 1994. In this way, editorial content parallels local reports of news out of Washington, which according to Graber has "a more local imprint . . . [to] make it more relevant to local audiences," compared to the reporting by the national media.[8]

I presume that the repetition of references to national political institutions and the themes that underlie these references ultimately affect how a significant segment of the public—editorial readers—view national politics. One assumes in most cases that editors and local political leaders share the same political space, interacting with each other in a number of venues and, more importantly, being exposed to similar points of view. The process is similar to what Gamson describes: "Each policy issue has a relevant public discourse—a particular set of ideas and symbols that are used in various public forums to construct meaning about it."[9] Editorials can play an important role in "constructing meaning" on matters they address.

Because editors and policymakers share a discourse community, editorial content in the daily newspaper is unlikely to catch the state and local political elite by surprise. The effect is more one of reinforcement of particular perceptions and themes, and that reinforcement has the potential of affecting how the public at large thinks of national politics.

STUDYING LOCAL MEDIA

Past studies of media content relevant to national political concerns have, for the most part, examined national media. Robinson and Sheehan looked at one national television network and a wire service.[10] Daniel Hallin built his work on media coverage of the Vietnam War in the *New York Times* and on network television news broadcasts.[11] More recently, Matthew Kerbel compared a traditional national network with a cable network.[12] Access to research material partially explains this focus. A theoretical reason carries more weight: the public has access to these national media, no matter where they live. Therefore, researchers can assume that media availability remains relatively constant across the nation.

Thomas Patterson was the among first of the modern scholars to augment an examination of national media content with that of local media in *The Mass Media Election*.[13] Just et al. skillfully combined a study of local media coverage with national media content in four different communities across the nation.[14] The logistics of a large-scale study of local media content across the nation, however, keeps most researchers from attempting the task.

The implicit assumption behind most studies is that media content relevant to national politics is best studied by examining national media outlets. This book does not question that assumption per se, but it suggests there are important limitations implied in such a presupposition and substantial value in going beyond the national media.

The differences among local newspapers in their editorial coverage represent one such advantage. Although this study did not systematically explore variations among the ten papers because the purpose was to develop the themes that emerge from the editorials as a whole, some summary comments about the variety reflected among the papers may be in order.

As already noted in chapter 2, the larger the paper, the more editorials dealing with national politics it ran. The Fresno and Providence dailies, for instance, resembled the *New York Times* and the *Washington Post* more than they did the other papers in the study, in the number and subjects of their editorials. The smaller newspapers varied considerably, with *Lansing State Journal* readers rarely encountering an editorial addressing national political affairs.

Several papers displayed preferences for some editorial topics to a greater extent than other editors did. For instance, the *Lexington Herald-Leader* rode the "ethics in government" hobbyhorse all year, but especially during the Kentucky state legislative session when several ethics bills were being considered. For the *Lansing State Journal*, the proposed downtown redevelopment sparked numerous editorials, and in true booster spirit, they had a favorable tone. The possible expansion of the Mountain Home Air Force Base training range captured a great deal of editorial attention in the *Boise Idaho Statesman*. Adding the *Jackson Clarion-Ledger*'s emphasis on crime in 1994, four of the ten newspapers focused more than casual attention on one topic each.

If one were to arrange these ten papers on a liberal to conservative continuum, the paper furthest to the right would be the *Boise Idaho Statesman*. It took the most strident position on investigating Whitewater early in the year, and it repeatedly supported lower government spending and less federal government action. The *Jackson Clarion-Ledger* tended toward the conservative end of the spectrum, in large part because of its continuing emphasis on crime as a social problem, both nationally and locally. On other issues, the editors straddled the middle most of the time.

Fresno readers were given larger doses of more liberal editorials than those in other papers. The editors were open to new governmental programs to combat societal problems, including Clinton's health-care proposal. They were more hesitant in supporting both the crime bill and welfare reform. The editors ranked preventing crime higher than fighting it, and they worried that people who needed help would be unable to get it because of a push to reduce welfare dependence generally. Raleigh editorials were only somewhat less liberal than those appearing in the *Bee.*

IDEOLOGY AND PARTISANSHIP

The editors did not blatantly flaunt their political orientation. One searches in vain for phrases such as, "Consistent with the generally conservative position this paper has taken, we now. . . ." The orientation surfaces more in the selection of examples that illustrates the editors' messages and in the accommodations in principles they are willing to make. More conservative editors, for example, may only be more willing to accept greater governmental regulation if it helps attain an outcome with which they agree, while more liberal editors may not even question the need for the regulation.

That said, one should recognize that ideological references appeared very rarely in any of these editorials. Editors discussed congressional squabbles in terms of cumbersome and disliked procedures, but not as instances of a conservative–liberal split among members. Bureaucratic regulations came under fire because they caused difficulties and seemed illogical, not because they were products of a federal government tilted toward liberalism. Even in discussions about the import of the Republican congressional victory in November, editors were inclined to draw a contrast between the role of critic the GOP had become used to and its new role of being in the majority, rather than see the result in ideological terms.

Perhaps, had we examined editorials in 1995 when the national government was divided between a Democratic president in the White House and a Republican majority in Congress, we might have found editors applying greater ideological characterizations to national politics. The rarity of ideological references, then, may very well be a product of the time period chosen for analysis, always a risk when a study is restricted to one year. Nevertheless, their absence is real and worth noting.

As surprising as the absence of ideology in editorial commentary is the virtual lack of references to parties as a way to help readers make sense out of national politics. Party labels served merely as a way to identify political leaders. Editors did not use them as a way to account for cooperation among some or for conflict among other officials. Neither did they use the labels regularly to distinguish Democrats and their policy preferences from Republicans and theirs. The exceptions occurred generally in commentary on various pieces of legislation moving through Congress, and even then editors applied partisan references only occasionally. Given editors' distaste for partisanship and party politics, one would have expected otherwise.

CONCLUSION

When local political elites consider policy options available to them, they necessarily take into account their own preferences, their own experiences, and their own constituencies. Debate about state or local policy choices reflects those concerns. This debate takes place not only in city council chambers, state legislative halls, or the governors' offices, but also in the community as a whole. Participants in this public discourse include active citizens as well as office holders.

These people all tend to read editorials regularly. When the editorials in the local daily newspaper express certain points of view, everyone knows that others, too, have encountered them. The points of view that editors advance then enter public discourse and have the opportunity to shape the local discussion of policy alternatives.

It is because of this potential impact on local public discourse that editorial commentary is a good way to examine local media's take on national politics. Editorials not only provide insight into editors' thinking, but because the thoughts are expressed in a forum that forms part of the common base of information for political activists, one can expect them to ultimately influence local public opinion.

If the content of newspaper editorials is a fair, if imperfect, indicator of public discourse in an area, then the amount of commentary on national issues the editorials examined here suggests that public discourse in these cities was neither parochial nor narrow, with the exception of Lansing. If a successfully functioning federal system presupposes a recognition of the relevance of other levels in the system, these editorials helped ensure that national perspectives were taken into account in state and local policy making. These editorials sent a strong signal to their readers that the national government matters in a direct rather than a remote way, and that state and local concerns are clearly connected to national policies and choices.

Despite the importance of proximity as a criterion of newsworthiness,[15] editors used scarce space in their opinion column to call attention to international and national issues and to place state and local concerns into a national context. How scarce is that resource? Few papers carried more than three editorials on any given day, and many ran only one or two. That there was as much commentary on national affairs, then, is a clear signal of the importance that editors placed on those events and a clear signal they are sending to their subscribers about the relative emphasis readers should give them as well.

The public discourse—stimulated by editorials such as these, drawing the connections between state and nation so frequently—is no doubt richer than it would be otherwise. State and local leaders have little political incentive to speak, positively or negatively, about national government programs. But editors can do so. They can make explicit the links between state and national interests, so that they are taken into account in discussions among citizens and among policymakers. It is the contribution editors make both to public discourse and to federalism in the United States.

The nation looks different from these ten cities than it does from inside the Beltway. From a national point of view, linkages to state policies and local concerns fade into insignificance. From the point of view of a local daily newspaper editor, these linkages are what it is all about. Without those connections, editors would only rarely write about national politics. These connections, however, present the crux of the matter for citizens across the nation. Editors help local readers see national events and institutions in the context of nearby concerns. The view from the states, then, is refracted through the prism of local priorities.

NOTES

1. "The Radiation Scandal," *Providence (Rhode Island) Journal*, 3 January 1994, 14(A).
2. "The Radiation Scandal."

3. John R. Hibbing and Elizabeth Theiss-Morse, "Process Preferences and American Politics: What the People Want Government to Be," *American Political Science Review* 95, no. 1 (March 2001): 151–52.

4. Paraphrasing Walter Lippman, *Public Opinion* (New York: Harcourt Brace, 1922), 358.

5. Jeffery J. Mondak, *Nothing to Read: Newspapers and Elections in a Social Experiment* (Ann Arbor: University of Michigan Press, 1995), 141 (italics added).

6. Mondak, *Nothing to Read*, 143.

7. Mondak, *Nothing to Read*, 166.

8. Doris A. Graber, *Mass Media and American Politics*, 5th ed. (Washington, D.C.: Congressional Quarterly, 1997), 328.

9. William A. Gamson, *Talking Politics* (New York: Cambridge University Press, 1992), 24.

10. Michael J. Robinson and Margaret A. Sheehan, *Over the Wire and On TV: CBS and UPI in Campaign '80* (New York: Russell Sage Foundation, 1983).

11. Daniel C. Hallin, *The "Uncensored War:" The Media and Vietnam* (New York: Oxford University Press, 1986).

12. Matthew Robert Kerbel, *Edited for Television: ABC, CNN, and the 1992 Presidential Election* (Boulder, Colo.: Westview Press, 1994).

13. Thomas E. Patterson, *The Mass Media Election* (New York: Praeger, 1980).

14. Marion R. Just et al., *Crosstalk: Citizens, Candidates, and the Media in a Presidential Campaign* (Chicago: University of Chicago Press, 1996).

15. Graber notes that proximity is "particularly important for newspapers." Doris A. Graber, *Mass Media and American Politics*, 4th ed. (Washington, D.C.: Congressional Quarterly, 1993), 120. For a contrary perspective, see Norman R. Luttbeg, "Proximity Does Not Assure Newsworthiness," *Journalism Quarterly* 60, no. 4 (winter 1983): 731–32.

Bibliography

Albany Times-Union, 26 January–25 December 1994.

Albuquerque (New Mexico) Journal, 4 January–15 December 1994.

Barber, James David. "Characters in the Campaign: The Literary Problem." In *Race for the Presidency: The Media and the Nominating Process*. Edited by James David Barber. Englewood Cliffs, N.J.: Prentice-Hall, 1978.

Bennett, W. Lance. "Toward a Theory of Press–State Relations in the United States." *Journal of Communication* 40, no. 2 (spring 1990): 103–25.

——. "An Introduction to Journalism Norms and Representation of Politics." *Political Communication* 13, no. 4 (October/December 1996): 373–84.

Bennett, W. Lance, and Timothy Cook, eds. "Journalism Norms and News Construction: Rules for Representing Politics." *Political Communication* 13, no. 4 (October/December 1996): 373–481.

Berkson, Larry C. *The Supreme Court and Its Publics*. Lexington, Mass.: Lexington Books, 1978.

Blumenthal, Sidney. "Letter from Washington: The Syndicated Presidency." *New Yorker*, 5 April 1993, 42–47.

Bogart, Leo. *Press and Public: Who Reads What, When, Where, and Why in American Newspapers*. 2nd ed. Hillsdale, N.J.: Lawrence Erlbaum, 1989.

Boise Idaho Statesman, 24 January–23 December 1994.

Bosso, Christopher J. "Setting the Agenda: Mass Media and the Discovery of Famine in Ethiopia." In *Manipulating Public Opinion: Essays on Public Opinion as a Dependent Variable*. Edited by Michael Margolis and Gary A. Mauser. Pacific Grove, Calif.: Brooks-Cole Publishing, 1989.

Caldeira, Gregory A. "Neither the Purse Nor the Sword: Dynamics of Public Confidence in the U.S. Supreme Court." *American Political Science Review* 80, no. 4 (December 1986): 1209–26.

Caldeira, Gregory A., and James L. Gibson. "The Etiology of Public Support for the Supreme Court." *American Journal of Political Science* 36, no. 3 (August 1992): 635–64.

Canes-Wrone, Brandice. "The President's Legislative Influence from Public Appeals." *American Journal of Political Science* 45, no. 2 (April 2001): 313–29.

Cantril, Albert H., and Susan Davis Cantril. *Reading Mixed Signals: Ambivalence in American Public Opinion about Government.* Washington, D.C.: Woodrow Wilson Center Press, 1999.

Cappella, Joseph N., and Kathleen Hall Jamieson. *Spiral of Cynicism: The Press and the Public Good.* New York: Oxford University Press, 1997.

Cohen, Bernard C. *The Press and Foreign Policy.* Princeton, N.J.: Princeton University Press, 1963.

Cohen, Jeffrey E., Jon R. Bond, Richard Fleisher, and John A. Hamman. "State-Level Presidential Approval and Senatorial Support." *Legislative Studies Quarterly* 25, no. 4 (November 2000): 577–90.

Conley, Richard S. "Unified Government, the Two Presidencies Thesis, and Presidential Support in the Senate: An Analysis of President Clinton's First Two Years." *Presidential Studies Quarterly* 27, no. 1 (spring 1997): 229–50.

Cook, Brian J. *Bureaucracy and Self-Government: Reconsidering the Role of Public Administration in American Politics.* Baltimore, Md.: Johns Hopkins University Press, 1996.

Cook, Timothy. *Making Laws & Making News: Media Strategies in the U.S. House of Representatives.* Washington, D.C.: Brookings Institution, 1989.

———. *Governing with the News: The News Media as a Political Institution.* Chicago: University of Chicago Press, 1998.

Cover, Albert D. "One Good Term Deserves Another: The Advantage of Incumbency in Congressional Elections." *American Journal of Political Science* 21, no. 3 (August 1977): 523–41.

Dalton, Russell J., Paul Allen Beck, and Robert Huckfeldt. "Partisan Cues and the Media: Information Flows in the 1992 Presidential Election." *American Political Science Review* 92, no. 1 (March 1998): 111–26.

Dalton, Russell J., Paul Allen Beck, Robert Huckfeldt, and William Koetzle. "A Test of Media-Centered Agenda Setting: Newspaper Content and Public Interests in a Presidential Election." *Political Communication* 15, no. 4 (October/December 1998): 463–81.

Davidson, Roger H., and Walter J. Oleszek. *Congress and Its Members.* 5th ed. Washington, D.C.: Congressional Quarterly, 1996.

Davis, Richard. *The Press and American Politics: The New Mediator.* New York: Longman, 1992.

———. *Decisions and Images: The Supreme Court and the Press*. Englewood Cliffs, N.J.: Prentice-Hall, 1994.

Delli Carpini, Michael X., and Scott Keeter. *What Americans Know About Politics and Why It Matters*. New Haven, Conn.: Yale University Press, 1996.

Demers, David. "Corporate Newspaper Structure, Editorial Page Vigor and Social Courage." *Journalism and Mass Communication Quarterly* 73, no. 4 (winter 1996): 857–77.

Dodds, Graham G., and Mark J. Rozell. "The Press and the Presidency: Then and Now." In *The Presidency: Then and Now*. Edited by Philip G. Henderson. Lanham, Md.: Rowman & Littlefield, 2000.

Dragoo, Kathleen, Melissa Duits, and William Haltom. "Reconsidering the Nagel-Erikson Hypothesis: Editorial Reactions to Church–State Cases." *American Politics Quarterly*, 21, no. 3 (June 1993): 368–78.

Editor and Publisher. "Wire Services Pick Top Stories of 1994." *Editor and Publisher*, 7 January 1995, 54.

Edwards, George C. III, *Presidential Influence in Congress*. San Francisco: W. H. Freeman and Company, 1980.

———. "Building Coalitions." *Presidential Studies Quarterly* 30, no. 1 (March 2000): 47–78.

Edwards, George C. III, and B. Dan Wood. "Who Influences Whom? The President, Congress, and the Media." *American Political Science Review* 93, no. 2 (June 1999): 327–44.

Elezar, Daniel J. *American Federalism: A View from the States*. 2nd ed. New York: Thomas Y. Crowell Company, 1972.

Elving, Ronald E. "Brighter Lights, Wider Windows: Presenting Congress in the 1990s." In *Congress, the Press, and the Public*. Edited by Thomas E. Mann and Norman J. Ornstein. Washington, D.C.: American Enterprise Institute and Brookings Institution, 1994.

Entman, Robert M. *Democracy Without Citizens: Media and the Decay of American Politics*. New York: Oxford University Press, 1989.

Epstein, Lee, and Jeffrey S. Segal, "Measuring Issue Salience." *American Journal of Political Science* 44, no. 1 (January 2000): 66–83.

Erbring, Lutz, Edie N. Goldenberg, and Arthur H. Miller. "Front-Page News and Real-World Cues: A New Look at Agenda-Setting by the Media." *American Journal of Political Science* 24, no. 1 (February 1980): 16–49.

Ericson, David. "Newspaper Coverage of the Supreme Court: A Case Study." *Journalism Quarterly* 54, no. 3 (autumn 1977): 605–7.

Erikson, Robert S. "The Influence of Newspaper Endorsements in Presidential Elections." *American Journal of Political Science* 20, no. 2 (May 1976): 207–33.

Fan, David P. *Predictions of Public Opinion from the Mass Media*. Westport, Conn.: Greenwood Press, 1988.

Fenno, Richard F. Jr. "If, as Ralph Nader Says, Congress Is 'The Broken Branch,' How Come We Love Our Congressmen So Much?" In *Congress and Change: Evolution and Reform.* Edited by Norman J. Ornstein. New York: Praeger, 1975.

Fresno (California) Bee, 4 January–31 December 1994.

Funston, Richard. *A Vital National Seminar: The Supreme Court in American Political Life.* Palo Alto, Calif.: Mayfield, 1978.

Gamson, William A. *Talking Politics.* New York: Cambridge University Press, 1992.

Gates, Melissa, and Jan P. Vermeer. "Reporting Supreme Court Decisions: Conflict, Dissents, and Other Cues." Paper presented at the annual meeting of the Western Political Science Association, San Francisco, Calif., March 1992.

Glendening, Parris N., and Mavis Mann Reeves. *Pragmatic Federalism: An Intergovernmental View of American Government.* Pacific Palisades, Calif.: Palisades Publishing, 1977.

Goldenberg, Edie N., and Michael W. Traugott. "Mass Media Effects on Recognizing and Rating Candidates in U.S. Senate Elections." In *Campaigns in the News: Mass Media and Congressional Elections.* Edited by Jan Pons Vermeer. Westport, Conn.: Greenwood Press, 1987.

Gonzalez, Noelle. "Editorials and Evaluations of Presidents: Public Expectations of Incumbent Presidents and Retrospective Voting." Paper presented at the annual meeting of the Midwest Political Science Association, Chicago, Ill., April 1994.

Goodsell, Charles T. *The Case for Bureaucracy: A Public Administration Polemic.* 3rd ed. Chatham, N.J.: Chatham House, 1994.

Graber, Doris A. *Mass Media and American Politics.* 4th ed. Washington, D.C.: Congressional Quarterly, 1993.

———. *Mass Media and American Politics.* 5th ed. Washington, D.C.: Congressional Quarterly, 1997.

Gregg, James E. "Newspaper Editorial Endorsements and California Elections." *Journalism Quarterly* 42, no. 3 (autumn 1964): 532–38.

Grossman, Michael Baruch, and Martha Joynt Kumar. *Portraying the President: The White House and the News Media.* Baltimore, Md.: Johns Hopkins University Press, 1981.

Hallin, Daniel C. *The "Uncensored War": The Media and Vietnam.* New York: Oxford University Press, 1986.

Herbst, Susan. *Reading Public Opinion: How Political Actors View the Democratic Process.* Chicago: University of Chicago Press, 1998.

Hess, Stephen. *The Government/Press Connection.* Washington, D.C.: Brookings Institution, 1984.

Hibbing, John, and Elizabeth Theiss-Morse. *Congress as Public Enemy.* Cambridge, Mass.: Cambridge University Press, 1995.

———. "Process Preferences and American Politics: What the People Want Government to Be." *American Political Science Review* 95, no. 1 (March 2001): 145–53.

Hinckley, Barbara. *Congressional Elections*. Washington, D.C.: Congressional Quarterly, 1978.

Hoekstra, Valerie J. "The Supreme Court and Local Public Opinion." *American Political Science Review* 94, no. 1 (March 2000): 89–100.

Hurd, Robert E., and Michael W. Singletary. "Newspaper Influence on the 1980 Presidential Election Vote." *Journalism Quarterly* 61, no. 2 (summer 1985): 332–38.

Hynds, Ernest C. "Editorial Pages Are Taking Stands, Providing Forums." *Journalism Quarterly* 53, no. 3 (autumn 1976): 532–35.

———. "Editorials, Opinion Pages Still Have Vital Roles at Most Newspapers." *Journalism Quarterly* 61, no. 3 (autumn 1984): 634–39.

Hynds, Ernest C., and Erika Archibald. "Improved Editorial Pages Can Help Papers' Communities." *Newspaper Research Journal* 17, no. 1-2 (winter/spring 1996): 14–24.

Hynds, Ernest C., and Charles H. Martin. "Editorial Writers Tell How They Go about Their Work." *Journalism Quarterly* 54, no. 4 (winter 1978): 776–69.

Jackson (Mississippi) Clarion-Ledger, 2 January–13 December 1994.

Jacobson, Gary C. *The Politics of Congressional Elections*. 4th ed. New York: Longman, 1997.

Jacobson, Gary C., and Samuel Kernell. *Strategy and Choice in Congressional Elections*. New Haven, Conn.: Yale University Press, 1981.

Jamieson, Kathleen Hall, and Karlyn Kohrs Campbell. *The Interplay of Influence: Mass Media & Their Publics in News, Advertising, Politics*. Belmont, Calif.: Wadsworth, 1983.

Jasperson, Amy E., Dhavan V. Shah, Mark Watts, Ronald J. Faber, and David P. Fan. "Framing and the Public Agenda: Media Effects on the Importance of the Federal Budget Deficit." *Political Communication* 15, no. 2 (April/June 1998): 205–24.

Jennings, M. Kent. "Ideological Thinking among Mass Publics and Political Elites." *Public Opinion Quarterly* 56, no. 4 (winter 1992): 419–41.

Johnson, Charles A., and Bradley C. Canon. *Judicial Policies: Implementation and Impact*. Washington, D.C.: Congressional Quarterly, 1984.

Johnson, Michelle, Keith Stamm, Joanne Lisosky, and Jeanette James. "Differences among Newspapers in Contributions to Knowledge of National Public Affairs." *Newspaper Research Journal* 13, no. 3 (summer 1995): 82–95.

Jones, Charles O. *The Presidency in a Separated System*. Washington, D.C.: Brookings Institution, 1994.

Just, Marion R., Ann N. Crigler, Dean E. Alger, Timothy E. Cook, Montague Kern, and Darrell M. West. *Crosstalk: Citizens, Candidates, and the Media in a Presidential Campaign*. Chicago: University of Chicago Press, 1996.

Kaniss, Phyllis. *Making Local News*. Chicago: University of Chicago Press, 1991.

Keiser, Lael R., and Joe Soss. "With Good Cause: Bureaucratic Discretion and the Politics of Child Support Enforcement." *American Journal of Political Science* 42, no. 4 (October 1998): 1133–56.

Kerbel, Matthew Robert. *Edited for Television: ABC, CNN, and the 1992 Presidential Election.* Boulder, Colo.: Westview Press, 1994.

Kernell, Samuel. *Going Public: New Strategies of Presidential Leadership.* Washington, D.C.: Congressional Quarterly, 1986.

Key, V. O. Jr. *Public Opinion and American Democracy.* New York: Alfred A. Knopf, 1961.

Kinsey, Dennis F., and Steven H. Chaffee. "Communication Behavior and Presidential Approval: The Decline of George Bush." *Political Communication* 13, no. 3 (July/September 1996): 281–91.

Knott, Jack H., and Gary J. Miller. *Reforming Bureaucracy: The Politics of Institutional Choice.* Englewood Cliffs, N.J.: Prentice-Hall, 1987.

Kosaki, Liane C., and Charles H. Franklin. "Public Awareness of Supreme Court Decisions." Paper presented at the annual meeting of the Midwest Political Science Association, Chicago, Ill., April 1991.

Krosnick, Jon A., and Laura A. Brannon. "New Evidence on News Media Priming: In 1992, It Was the Economy!" Paper presented at the annual meeting of the American Political Science Association, Chicago, Ill., 1995.

Lacy, Stephen. "Competition among Metropolitan Daily, Small Daily and Weekly Newspapers. *Journalism Quarterly* 61, no. 3 (autumn 1984): 640–44, 742.

Lansing (Michigan) State Journal, 23 July–10 November, 1994.

Larson, Stephanie Greco. "How the New York *Times* Covered Discrimination Cases." *Journalism Quarterly* 62, no. 4 (winter 1985): 894–96.

Lenart, Silvo. *Shaping Political Attitudes: The Impact of Interpersonal Communication and Mass Media.* Thousand Oaks, Calif.: Sage Publications, 1994.

Lexington (Kentucky) Herald-Leader, 26 January–26 November 1994.

Lincoln (Nebraska) Journal, 10 January–29 December 1994.

Lippmann, Walter. *Public Opinion.* New York: Harcourt Brace, 1922.

Lowi, Theodore. *The Personal President.* Ithaca, N.Y.: Cornell University Press, 1985.

Luttbeg, Norman R. "Proximity Does Not Assure Newsworthiness." *Journalism Quarterly* 60, no. 4 (winter 1983): 731–32.

Mann, Thomas E., and Norman J. Ornstein, eds. *Congress, the Press, and the Public.* Washington, D.C.: American Enterprise Institute and Brookings Institution, 1994.

Martin, Paul. "Over the Wire and Then What?" Paper presented at the annual meeting of the Midwest Political Science Association, Chicago, Ill., April 1996.

Maslin-Wicks, Kimberly. "Two Types of Presidential Influence in Congress." *Presidential Studies Quarterly* 28, no. 1 (winter 1998): 108–26.

McCombs, Maxwell E., and Donald L. Shaw. "The Agenda-Setting Function of Mass Media." *Public Opinion Quarterly* 36, no. 2 (summer 1972): 176–87.

Misciagno, Patricia S. "Rethinking the Mythic Presidency." *Political Communication* 13, no. 3 (July/September 1996): 329–44.

Moen, Matthew C., and Gary W. Copeland. *The Contemporary Congress: A Bicameral Approach*. Belmont, Calif.: West/Wadsworth, 1999.

Mondak, Jeffery J. *Nothing to Read: Newspapers and Elections in a Social Experiment*. Ann Arbor: University of Michigan Press, 1995.

Morgan, David. *The Flacks of Washington: Government Information and the Public Agenda*. Westport, Conn.: Greenwood Press, 1986.

Murphy, Walter F., and C. Herman Pritchett. *Courts, Judges, and Politics: An Introduction to the Judicial Process*. 4th ed. New York: Random House, 1986.

Myers, David S. "Editorials and Foreign Affairs in Recent Presidential Campaigns." *Journalism Quarterly* 59, no. 4 (winter 1982): 541–47.

Neubauer, David W. *Judicial Process: Law, Courts, and Politics in the United States*. Belmont, Calif.: Brooks/Cole Publishing Company, 1991.

Neustadt, Richard E. *Presidential Power and the Modern Presidents: The Politics of Leadership from Roosevelt to Reagan*. New York: Free Press, 1990.

Oliver, J. Eric. "City Size and Civic Involvement in Metropolitan America." *American Political Science Review* 94, no. 2 (June 2000): 361–73.

Page, Benjamin I., Robert Y. Shapiro, and Glenn R. Dempsey. "What Moves Public Opinion?" *American Political Science Review* 81, no. 1 (March 1987): 23–43.

Paletz, David. *The Media in American Politics: Contents and Consequences*. New York: Longman, 1999.

Patterson, Thomas E. *The Mass Media Election*. New York: Praeger, 1980.

Postman, Neil. *Amusing Ourselves to Death: Public Discourse in the Age of Show Business*. New York: Viking, 1985.

Powell, Lewis F. Jr. "What Really Goes On at the Supreme Court." In *Judges on Judging: Views from the Bench*. Edited by David M. O'Brien. Chatham, N.J.: Chatham House Publishers, 1997.

Providence (Rhode Island) Journal, 3 January–16 December 1994.

Raleigh (North Carolina) News and Observer, 8 January–30 December 1994.

Ripley, Randall B., and Grace A. Franklin. *Congress, the Bureaucracy, and Public Policy*. 3rd ed. Homewood, Ill.: Dorsey Press, 1984.

Robinson, Michael J. "Three Faces of Congressional Media." In *The New Congress*. Edited by Thomas E. Mann and Norman J. Ornstein. Washington, D.C.: American Enterprise Institute, 1981.

Robinson, Michael J., and Margaret A. Sheehan. *Over the Wire and On TV: CBS and UPI in Campaign '80*. New York: Russell Sage Foundation, 1983.

Roshco, Bernard. *Newsmaking*. Chicago: University of Chicago Press, 1975.

Rossiter, Clinton. *The American Presidency*. Revised edition. New York: Harcourt, Brace & World, 1960.

Rozell, Mark J. "Press Coverage of Congress, 1946–92." In *Congress, the Press, and the Public*. Edited by Thomas E. Mann and Norman J. Ornstein.

Washington, D.C.: American Enterprise Institute and Brookings Institution, 1994.

———. "Presidential Image-Makers on the Limits of Spin Control." *Presidential Studies Quarterly* 25, no. 1 (winter 1995): 67–90.

St. Dizier, Byron. "The Effect of Newspaper Endorsements and Party Identification on Voting Choice." *Journalism Quarterly* 62, no. 3 (autumn 1985): 589–94.

Schaefer, Todd M. "Persuading the Persuaders: Presidential Speeches and Editorial Opinion." *Political Communication* 14, no. 1 (January/March 1997): 97–111.

Schiller, Dan. *Objectivity and the News: The Public and the Rise of Commercial Journalism.* Philadelphia: University of Pennsylvania Press, 1981.

Scholz, John T., and B. Dan Wood. "Controlling the IRS: Principals, Principles, and Public Administration." *American Journal of Political Science* 42, no. 1 (January 1998): 141–62.

Schudson, Michael. *Discovering the News: A Social History of American Newspapers.* New York: Basic Books, 1978.

Segal, Jeffrey A., and Albert D. Cover. "Ideological Values and the Votes of U.S. Supreme Court Justices." *American Political Science Review* 83, no. 2 (June 1989): 557–66.

Segal, Jeffrey A., and Harold J. Spaeth. *The Supreme Court and the Attitudinal Model.* Cambridge, Mass.: Cambridge University Press, 1993.

Simon, Dennis M., and Charles W. Ostrom Jr. "The Politics of Prestige: Popular Support and the Modern Presidency." *Presidential Studies Quarterly,* 18, no. 4 (fall 1988): 741–59.

Slotnick, Elliot E., and Jennifer A. Segal. "Television News and the Supreme Court." Paper presented at the annual meeting of the American Political Science Association, Chicago, Ill., September 1992.

Smoller, Frederick T. *The Six O'Clock Presidency: A Theory of Presidential Press Relations in the Age of Television.* New York: Praeger, 1990.

Solimine, Michael. "Newsmagazine Coverage of the Supreme Court." *Journalism Quarterly* 57, no. 4 (winter 1980): 661–63.

Stuckey, Mary E. *The President as Interpreter-in-Chief.* Chatham, N.J.: Chatham House Publishers, 1991.

Tulis, Jeffrey K. *The Rhetorical Presidency.* Princeton, N.J.: Princeton University Press, 1987.

Vermeer, Jan Pons. *"For Immediate Release": Candidate Press Releases in American Political Campaigns.* Westport, Conn.: Greenwood Press, 1982.

———, ed. *Campaigns in the News: Mass Media and Congressional Elections.* Westport, Conn.: Greenwood Press, 1987.

———. "Themes in Local Newspaper Editorials: Newsworthiness and Editorial Commentary." Paper presented at the annual meeting of the Southwest Political Science Association, Dallas, Tex., March 1995.

Vogler, David J. *The Politics of Congress*. 6th ed. Madison, Wis.: Brown and Benchmark Publishers, 1993.

Walker, David B. *The Rebirth of Federalism: Slouching toward Washington.* Chatham, N.J.: Chatham House Publishing, 1995.

Waterman, Richard, and Gerald Wright. *The "Image Is Everything" Presidency*. Boulder, Colo.: Westview Press, 1999.

Wildavsky, Aaron. "The Two Presidencies." *Trans-Action* 4, no. 2 (December 1966): 7–14.

Wolfsfeld, Gadi. "Fair Weather Friends: The Varying Role of the News Media in the Arab–Israeli Peace Process." *Political Communication* 14, no. 1 (January/March 1997): 29–48.

Zaller, John. *The Nature and Origins of Mass Opinion*. New York: Cambridge University Press, 1992.

Index

Afghanistan, 14
Agriculture, 116, 122
Agriculture, U.S. Department of, 81, 85, 90–92
Agenda-setting, 3–4, 7, 36, 76n7
Air quality, 86
Albany, New York, 14
Albany Times-Union, 28, 35, 47; Breyer, Stephen, 105; bureaucracy, 89–92; Central Intelligence Agency, 92–93; Clinton, 60, 71, 73; and Congress, 47–48, 51–52, 68; endorsements, 44; Federal Bureau of Investigation, 88; Ideology, 112n37; Haiti, 21, 67; Supreme Court, 106–7, 110; water quality, 118–19; Albuquerque, New Mexico, 14
Albuquerque Journal: bureaucracy, 90; Clinton, 73; and Congress, 47; congressional elections, 2; crime bill, 39, 52; Environmental Protection Agency, 89; ethics, 92; Federalism, 120–21, 124; grazing

fees, 87; gun control, 40; Haiti, 67–69; Helms, Jesse, 46; immigration, 37; Supreme Court, 101, 105–6; water quality, 86; Whitewater, 71–72; Ames, Aldrich, 92–93; AMTRAK, 118
Ariste, Jean-Betrand, 21, 67
Associated Press, 31–32, 34, 36, 63, 103. *See also* Wire services
Audience concerns, 16
"Audience-driven" topic selection, 25–26, 28, 35–36, 132

Babbitt, Bruce, 87
Balkans, 2. *See also* Bosnia, Serbia
Barber, James David, 65–66, 78n37
Baseball strike, 36
Batt, Phil, 125
Beck, Paul A., 11, 19n39
Beilenson, Tony, 45
Bennett, W. Lance, 23, 38nn8–9
Bereuter, Douglas K., 44
Bingaman, Jeff, 45
Blackmun, Harry F., 104–6, 133

Blumenthal, Sidney, 7–8, 18n25, 63, 78n32
Bogart, Leo, 8, 18nn30–31
Boise, Idaho, 14
Boise Idaho Statesman: bureaucracy, 81, 87, 136; and Congress, 39, 45, 50, 120–21; endorsements, 44; federalism, 115, 119, 124; grazing fees, 37; and president, 59, 67, 73; Supreme Court, 107; "unfunded mandates," 121–22; Whitewater, 71
Bosnia, 1–2, 31, 33, 36, 59, 66
Boston, Massachusetts, 14
Brady Law, 40. *See also* gun control
Breyer, Stephen, 104–5, 133
Bureaucracy, 2, 16, 26, 29–30, 34, 64, 95n7, 100, 133–34; and clientele groups, 41; and health-care reform, 50; individual bureaucrats, 90–93; media coverage of, 84–85; public opinion of, 61–63. *See also* specific agencies
Bush, George, 68
Bush, George W., xi

Cabinet, 65. *See also* individual departments
Caldeira, Gregory A., 102, 111nn6–7
California, 116, 124
California Public Utilities Commission, 119
Campaign finance reform, 48
Campbell, Karlyn Kohrs, 6, 18n21
Canes-Wrone, Brandice, 62, 77n20
Canon, Bradley C., 102, 104, 108, 111n11, 112n24, 113n52
Cantril, Albert H., 126, 129n56
Cantril, Susan Davis, 126, 129n56
Cappella, Joseph N., 3, 17n7
Carlsbad Caverns, 45
Carter, Jimmy, 1, 21, 68
Casey, William, 84

Cedras, Raoul, 21, 59, 67–68
Central Intelligence Agency, 84, 92–93
Chaffee, Steven H., 62, 77n21
China, 66
Churchill, Winston, 99
Circulation of newspapers, 14, 26–29, 31, 33–35, 37, 136
Clientele groups, 82–83. *See also* interest groups, special interest groups
Clinton, Hillary, 59
Clinton administration, 2, 31, 109–10
Clinton, Bill, 7, 21, 36, 46, 49–52, 59–60, 63–64, 66–76, 91, 105, 132; Whitewater, 1, 31, 33–34, 36, 50, 59, 65–66, 70–73, 75–76, 136
Cohen, Bernard C., 36, 38n15
Cohen, Jeffrey E., 62, 77n17
Commerce, U.S. Department of, 86
Commission on Immigration Reform, 89
Condit, Gary, 4
Congress, U.S., xii, 2, 12, 16, 25–26, 29–31, 60, 73–74, 84–85, 90, 92, 100, 121, 123–24, 132; bureaucracy, 83; crime bill, 1, 15, 31, 33, 36, 39, 45, 49, 51–53, 59, 66, 69, 72, 137–138; health-care reform, 1, 15, 47, 19–51, 59, 66, 69, 71–73; federalism, 117, 120; foreign affairs, 68–69; gun control, 51–52; and news, 3, 42–43, 53–55, 60, 103; and president, 64–66, 69–70, 74–76, 132–33; and presidential approval, 61–62; public perceptions of, 39–43, 81; welfare reform, 1, 66, 69–70, 137; Whitewater, 71–72
Congress, U.S., members of, 7–8, 16, 35, 39, 42–47, 54, 62, 64, 66, 72, 92, 100, 126, 132

Jamieson, Kathleen Hall, 3, 6, 17n7,
  18n21
Jasperson, Amy E., 4, 17n14
Johnson, Charles A., 102, 104, 108,
  111n11, 112n24, 113n52
Jones, Brereton, 123
Jones, Charles O., 62, 77n13
Jones, Paula Corbin, 71
Joint Committee on the Organization
  of Congress, 47
Just, Marion, 13, 20n56, 136,
  140n14
Justice, U.S. Department of, 120

Kaniss, Phyllis, 13, 19n37
Kansas City, Missouri, 109
Keeter, Scott, 12, 20n54, 61, 77n9
Kempthorne, Dirk, 45, 122
Kentucky, 7, 109, 123
Kerbel, Matthew R., 135, 140n12
Kernell, Samuel, 61, 76n8
Kerrigan, Nancy, 36
Key, V. O. Key Jr., 4, 17n12
Kinsey, Dennis F., 62, 77n21
Koop, C. Everett, 85
Kosaki, Liane C., 110, 113n60
Kuwait, 92

Labor, U.S. Department of, 86
Lacy, Stephen, 9, 19n33
Land use, 37. *See also* grazing fees
Lansing, Michigan, 14, 28, 139
Lansing State Journal, 7, 21, 28, 33,
  71, 132, 136; and Congress, 48,
  51–52; federalism, 119; water
  quality, 87
LaRocco, Larry, 44
Legislative process, 70
Lexington, Kentucky, 14, 31
Lexington Herald-Leader, 26, 33, 60,
  136; and bureaucracy, 89;
  circulation, 33, 35; crime bill, 52;
  Haiti, 68; Helms, Jesse, 46; and
  president, 73; Supreme Court,

105, 107; tobacco, 3, 37, 122–23,
  126; "unfunded mandates," 40
Lincoln, Nebraska, 81
Lincoln Journal, 30; bureaucrats,
  91–92; and bureaucracy, 45, 81,
  88; circulation, 14, 26; and
  Congress, 47, 50; crime bill, 52;
  endorsements, 44; federalism, 12;
  gun control, 118; Haiti, 67–68;
  and Supreme Court, 105, 109;
  "unfunded mandates," 121–22;
  water quality, 86, 119;
  Whitewater, 71
Lippmann, Walter, 24, 38n10
Los Alamos, New Mexico, 85
Los Angeles, California, 8
Los Angeles Times, 8
Lott, Trent, 44

Madisonian system, 64–65
Martin, Paul, 2, 8, 13–14, 17n5,
  18n27, 20n58
Massachusetts, 131
Maslin-Wicks, Kimberly, 62, 77n16
McNulty, Michael, 44
Medicaid, 121
Mescalero Apaches, 125
Miami Herald, 6
Michigan, 116, 132
Middle East, 1, 3, 31, 66
Misciagno, Patricia S., 62, 77n15
Mississippi, 9, 118–19
Mitchell, George, 40, 51
Mondak, Jeffery J., 14, 20n60,
  134–35, 140n5
Morgan, David, 84, 95n13
Montana, 109
Mountain Home Air Force Base, 136
Murphy, Walter F., 102, 111n10
Myers, David, 11–12, 19n42

*National Organization for Women v.
  Scheidler*, 106
National Reconnaissance Office, 89

National Rifle Association, 51
National Weather Service, 82
National-local connections, 7, 11, 16, 27–28, 30–31, 34–35, 100, 108–10, 117, 125–26, 134–35, 139
Nebraska, 88, 109
"Necessary and proper" clause, 125
Nelson, Ben, 121
Neustadt, Richard, 61, 77n10
New Deal, 122
New Mexico, 86–87, 124–25
New York City, 14
New York Times, 5, 63, 135–36
News, 2–3
Newsmagazines, 13
Newsweek, 5
Newsworthiness, 3, 16, 23–24, 26, 35, 84–85, 95n14, 103; proximity as newsworthiness criterion, 10, 46, 85, 139, 140n15
News beats, 84
News content, 4, 8
"News-driven" topic selection, xii, 25–26, 28, 33, 35–36, 132
NIMBY, 124–25
Northridge, California, earthquake, 36
North Carolina, 9, 88, 109, 123
North Korea, 1, 31, 33, 59, 66
Nuclear waste, 115, 125
Nunn, Sam, 21, 68

Objectivity, 5, 22–23, 72, 103
Occupational Safety and Health Administration (OSHA), 93
Oleszek, Walter J., 48, 53, 57n47, 58n80
O'Neill, Thomas P. ("Tip"), 14
Opinion leadership, 5, 10
Oversight, 92
Oxford model of debate, 47

Paletz, David, 84, 95n10, 103, 113n22
Panama, 45
Park Service, U.S., 121
Partisanship, 39, 46–48, 51, 54, 71, 137–38
Pastor, Robert, 45
Patterson, Thomas, 136, 140n13
Philadelphia, Pennsylvania, 13
Political parties, 138. *See also* Democrats, Republicans
Pork barrel legislation, 41, 46–47, 52, 54
Postal Service, U.S., 82
Postman, Neil, 37, 38n16
Powell, Colin, 21, 68
Powell, Lewis F. Jr., 103, 112n20
Pragmatic federalism, 16, 120, 122, 125–26, 133–34. *See also* federalism
Presidency, 16, 41, 60–76, 99
President, 7, 12, 25–26, 29–31, 34, 83, 85, 103
Presidential elections, 4, 14
Pritchett, C. Herman, 102, 111n10
Providence, Rhode Island, 14, 26, 50
Providence Journal, 14, 22, 30; Blackmun, Harry F., 104; bureaucracy, 88–90, 131; circulation, 26, 35–36; Clinton, 73; crime bill, 53; Haiti, 67–68; Hastings, Alcee, 46; Supreme Court, 107; "unfunded mandates," 121; Whitewater, 71–72
Public discourse, xiii, 6–8, 11–13, 37, 64, 74, 126, 132–35, 138–39
Public information officers, 84
Public opinion, 6, 10–11, 60, 117, 122, 127n8, 138
Puerto Rico, 46

Raleigh, North Carolina, 14, 31
Raleigh News & Observer, 22, 28, 137; bureaucracy, 86, 89–90; Central Intelligence Agency, 93; circulation, 33; and Congress, 39,

About the Author

Jan P. Vermeer is professor of political science at Nebraska Wesleyan University. He is the author of *"For Immediate Release": Candidate Press Releases in American Political Campaigns* (Greenwood Press, 1982), and the editor of *Campaigns in the News: Mass Media and Congressional Elections* (Greenwood Press, 1987) and *In "Media" Res: Readings in Mass Media and American Politics* (McGraw-Hill, 1995).